D0260911

Visions of England

Visions of England

ROY STRONG

GLOUCESTERSHIRE COUNTY COUNCIL	
9933843710	
Bertrams	21/07/2011
AN	£17.99
GL	

THE BODLEY HEAD
LONDON

Published by The Bodley Head 2011

2 4 6 8 10 9 7 5 3 1

Copyright © Roy Strong 2011

Roy Strong has asserted his right under the Copyright, Designs
and Patents Act 1988 to be identified as the author of this work

This book is sold subject to the condition that it shall not, by way of
trade or otherwise, be lent, resold, hired out, or otherwise
circulated without the publisher's prior consent in any form of binding
or cover other than that in which it is published and without a similar
condition, including this condition, being imposed on the subsequent purchaser

First published in Great Britain in 2011 by
The Bodley Head
Random House, 20 Vauxhall Bridge Road,
London SW1V 2SA

www.bodleyhead.co.uk
www.randomhouse.co.uk

Addresses for companies within The Random House Group Limited
can be found at:
www.randomhouse.co.uk/offices.htm

The Random House Group Limited Reg. No. 954009

A CIP catalogue record for this book
is available from the British Library

ISBN 9781847921604

The Random House Group Limited supports The Forest Stewardship
Council® (FSC®), the leading international forest certification organisation.
All our titles that are printed on Greenpeace approved FSC® certified
paper carry the FSC® logo. Our paper procurement policy can be found at:
www.randomhouse.co.uk/environment

Typeset in Bell by Palimpsest Book Production Limited,
Falkirk, Stirlingshire
Printed and bound in Great Britain by
Clays Ltd, St Ives plc

CONTENTS

Preface

This book is the latest in a series of publications, stretching over a decade and a half, in which I have tried to present our nation's past to a wide audience. This desire to communicate our history – in particular its creativity and astonishing immediacy – and how it has shaped our lives today has been the focus of my entire professional career. As director of the National Portrait Gallery and the Victoria & Albert Museum my guiding principle was to make our rich past available to everyman. That mission was often combined with alerting the public to the threat to some of our national icons; three landmark exhibitions which I staged in the 1970s concentrated on the history and uncertain future of our country houses, churches and gardens, triggering a huge response that helped ensure their survival.

My resignation from the V&A in 1987 signalled the end of my academic writing phase. I embarked on a series of books aimed to bring to life the nation's past and make it accessible to the largest possible readership. The first, *The Story of Britain* (1996), was written in response to the crisis in history teaching in our schools; the second, *The Spirit of Britain* (1999) – reissued as *The Arts in Britain* (2004) – attempted to sketch our rich cultural history. *Coronation* (2005) provided a fresh look at the monarchy, while *A Little History of the English*

Country Church (2007) told the story of these revered buildings and, with their survival under threat, presented a passionate plea for their preservation.

The present book was written with a similar sense of urgency. During the last decade there has been much public debate and a torrent of books on England and what it means to be English. This debate has often been politically charged, touching on highly controversial issues such as multiculturalism and devolution. *Visions of England* comes to the discussion from a different perspective: it examines how in the past the English have envisioned their country by means of literature, art, music and drama, and it asks whether this England of the imagination still speaks to us today. We need to understand where we come from in order to decide in which direction we want to go.

The text takes the form of a simple essay which I hope can be read in one sitting. However, this seemingly simple and short book has been quite a complex one to write and in achieving that, if indeed it has been achieved, I owe a huge debt to my editor Jörg Hensgen. His contribution has gone beyond the bounds of duty. Juliet Brightmore has yet again aided me in the search for telling images. And I must salute my literary agent, Felicity Bryan, for guiding me through this long succession of books, all of which have been written from the heart.

Roy Strong
The Laskett
March 2011

Introduction

What is England?

I WAS FOUR WHEN WAR broke out in 1939. That August we holidayed as a family at Caister in Norfolk: I can still remember the beach and our hurried departure back to London. I have few early memories of my two elder brothers as they were evacuated to East Anglia, taken in by farmers' families for the duration of the war. One of them, when he returned, did not recognise my mother; I can still recall the devastation of that moment.

During those years, our 1920s brick-terrace house in the north London suburbs became its own little island fortress. Both the front and the back gardens were turned into vegetable plots; where there had been a lawn and flower beds there were now neat rows of potatoes, carrots, leeks, tomatoes and salad greens. We kept chickens in a pen at the bottom of the garden, which gave us eggs and, at Christmas, the only roast bird of the year.

Inside the house we lived in two rooms: the kitchen in which we ate and the front living room which now held most of our furniture and belongings. One of the upstairs bedrooms stored a neighbour's furniture as he went off to fight. Across the windows were hung funereal swags of blackout curtaining; at night no chink of light was to be allowed to escape for fear of giving enemy aircraft a clue as to the humanity beneath. A latticework of sticky brown paper covered the windows, designed to avert the scattering of lethal shards of broken glass in the case of a bomb blast. In the dining room, sturdy wooden posts appeared to prevent the ceiling from collapsing and there, in an alcove formed by parts of an Anderson shelter, I slept. Outside, in the garden, there was the shelter itself to which, when the air-raid warning sounded, I was carried in my nightclothes.

The war in effect destroyed the family. Initially I was evacuated with my mother to the south coast, where I recall seeing holiday beaches covered with barbed wire. (Why we were sent to the very coast where the enemy would have landed is today beyond my reasoning.) Later we spent some time in East Anglia in a cottage lit by oil lamps before I was sent away on my own, a pathetic child with a label tied round my neck, to South Wales. I remember weeks of untold misery as I cried myself to sleep while the 'doodlebugs' fell on London.

As the war drew to its close my brothers and I returned home and a map of Europe was pinned to the living-room wall on which coloured pins recorded the gradual advance of the Allied forces into Germany. When the end finally came bonfires were piled high at the intersections of every street and there was laughter and tears. Yet the austerity and deprivation of those years would continue for another decade.

It is hardly surprising that the only occasion when the whole school was taken to see a film it was Laurence Olivier's production of *Henry V* (1944); it must have been in 1945, when I was ten. I can see it now in my mind's eye opening as it did in the playwright's Globe Theatre, but it quickly dissolves into a *Très Riches Heures* pasteboard world. This was a patriotic pageant with the great actor uttering those famous lines:

> On, on, you noblest English,
> Whose blood is set from fathers of war-proof!
> Fathers that, like so many Alexanders,
> Have in these parts from morn till even fought
> And sheathed their swords for lack of
>   argument:
> Dishonour not your mothers; now attest
> That those whom you call'd fathers did
>   beget you.
> Be copy now to men of grosser blood,
> And teach them how to war. And you, good
>   yeomen,
> Whose limbs were made in England, show
>   us here
> The mettle of your pasture; let us swear
> That you are worth your breeding; which I
>   doubt not;
> For there is none of you so mean and base,
> That hath no noble lustre in your eyes.
> I see you stand like greyhounds in the slips,
> Straining upon the start. The game's afoot:
> Follow your spirit, and upon this charge
> Cry 'God for Harry, England, and Saint George!'

*   *   *

I was taught history in the early 1950s, at a grammar school on the fastnesses of the Great Cambridge Road. At that time, and for decades after, it never crossed my mind that the history I learned about was wholly Anglocentric. I belong to the last generation that was taught what modern historians refer to as the Whig interpretation of the nation's past, that glorious progression from absolutism to parliamentary democracy. History was the history of England. Scotland, Wales and Ireland, if they came into it at all, only figured as incidentals to what was the triumphant story of an island people who came together to create a global empire, with a civilising mission in the form of our institutions, our law and our various democratic processes. There was no questioning the fact that England *was* Britain.

Today of course we do know that this isn't true. The empire has long become the Commonwealth and within the British Isles the Scottish and the Welsh have asserted their own identities, culminating in the establishment of a Scottish Parliament and a Welsh Assembly in 1999. Looking back, I now realise that I grew up during the last great imperial war, one in which the constituent parts of the United Kingdom together with its far-flung empire fought united against foes on the European mainland and in the Far East.

For many English people – and I am English by descent on both sides, with perhaps a smattering of Huguenot – this has come as a shock. We are suddenly forced to rediscover our own identity. That has not been a problem for either the Scots or the Welsh, who had to sharpen theirs over the centuries in reaction to the overwhelming dominance of the English on the island. The English face a more difficult problem: they have to disentangle England from Britain. That is not an easy task, for the two have been inextricably intertwined for so long that we have forgotten that they are in fact two quite distinct geographical and political entities.

The very act of devolution has meant that increasingly we are asked not to consider so much what we share as what sets us apart. I think it is significant that the 300th anniversary of the Act of Union in 2007 passed by largely unnoticed. And it seems to be symbolic that one of the Scotsman Gordon Brown's last acts as Chancellor of the Exchequer was finally to order the banishment of the figure of Britannia – who first appeared on second-century Roman coins – from the next issue of our coinage.

While Scottish and Welsh nationalism is generally regarded as a legitimate form of self-expression, those raising the flag for England are often labelled as chauvinist or racist. I find this baffling. One of the reasons I am proud of being English is the generosity of the country to all comers. England has always been a polyglot nation. The Anglo-Saxon kings styled themselves *rex Anglorum,* king of the Angles or English, although the realm also embraced Saxons and Jutes;

after 1066 William the Conqueror adopted the same title for his rule, which now included the Vikings and his own Norman followers. More important still, down the centuries England offered a home to those fleeing persecution – from the Huguenots in the sixteenth and seventeenth centuries to the Jews in the nineteenth – and after the dissolution of our empire in the 1950s and '60s, the country has welcomed immigrants from all parts of the world.

There has been widespread debate on Englishness and English identity in the media over the last few decades, and a huge amount of academic ink has been spilled deconstructing the island's identity and rewriting its history – in the process demolishing many of the old certainties I was brought up on. Yet while academics are good at dissecting and demolishing things, they usually don't regard it as their duty to replace what they have cheerfully knocked down; we are simply left with the debris. As far as I know, no one has attempted to describe for the wider reading public the iconography and mythology of England which *continue* to underwrite our national life in the twenty-first century. Moreover, while many are bemoaning what has been lost, little thought has been given to a reconfiguration of our identity. This book does not claim to offer a solution; instead I have tried to illuminate those traditions that remain building stones of Englishness in today's world.

In the process I have benefited a great deal from

the extremely valuable and perceptive scholarship of recent years; a select bibliography in the back of this little book is aimed at readers who want to explore some of the topics I raise here. From that scholarship we learn that the English have in effect defined themselves only twice: first between about 1580 and 1610 and then again between about 1880 and 1910.

During the Elizabethan era England became a Protestant nation. Shorn of any trace of its medieval continental empire it was now contained within the political boundaries we recognise today and the advent of cartography meant that for the first time English people could place themselves in the geographical space of the country. The Reformation and the break with Rome created a unique ecclesiastical system in the Church of England. From 1559 to 1829, the year of Catholic Emancipation, only members of the Church of England could hold any form of office or gain access to the two great universities. The Book of Common Prayer and the Authorised Version of the Bible provided a shared language and form of worship that defined the nation. England became the inviolate Protestant island whose people had defeated the might of Catholic Spain and in the following centuries laid low the forces of Catholic France. The Elizabethan period also witnessed a literary renaissance which exploded upon the scene during the last decade of the sixteenth century. English poets and playwrights created a vernacular literature the equal of that of ancient Greece and Rome, which is evident in the works of Sir Philip Sidney, Edmund Spenser, Michael Drayton, Christopher Marlowe, George Chapman, Sir Walter Raleigh and, above all, in the plays of William Shakespeare.

Much of this was drawn on in the late Victorian and Edwardian period, when a vision of the country was born that was to sustain the English people through two world wars and well into the twenty-first century. It celebrated the nation's old heartlands: the Anglo-Saxon kingdoms with their rolling countryside, their villages nestling in the valleys with their church spires rising above the surrounding buildings, their ancient manor houses, market towns and cathedral cities. This was a vision of England that was embraced by the Georgian poets, by painters such as John Piper and Paul Nash, and by a succession of composers ranging from Edward Elgar and Ralph Vaughan Williams to Benjamin Britten. This was the England that soldiers fought for in those world wars: they may have come from factories and offices yet they did not fight for Manchester or Birmingham but for the likes of Chipping Campden and Lavenham.

It is a striking fact that although England was the first industrialised country in Western Europe, where today eighty per cent of the population live in cities and towns, urban life forms no part of the iconography of England. As I will show, the reason for this is that by the time the Industrial Revolution began in the eighteenth century, English identity had already been framed in terms of the countryside. And as national identity exists primarily in the imagination, how could this vision of England's green and pleasant land be reconciled with the factories and furnaces, and the squalor and human degradation that came with it? While the countryside remains the touchstone of English identity, urban life seems to have been written out of our national iconography in an act of seemingly deliberate selectivity. It is similarly curious that although England is an island, whose commercial and imperial success depended for most of its history on its role as a great maritime power, the sea has never been at the heart of English identity. It too has never eclipsed the central role of the countryside.

Yet landscape runs through the centuries as an emblem of England not for its actuality but as a vehicle for a complex of ideas and emotions. As a key element in our national identity it has its roots in the England of Elizabeth I when Edmund Spenser and Sir Philip Sidney adapted the arcadia of the classical poets to this country and peopled it with their contemporaries. For poets such as Sir John Denham and Alexander Pope landscape evoked the nation's history; for painters like John Constable or J. M. W. Turner it was fused with personal memory. Most of all, landscape painting reflected the hopes and fears of the times; we only need to think of the rainbow of hope embracing Salisbury Cathedral in Constable's great painting executed just before the passing of the 1832 Reform Act. We can trace this trend through the twentieth century when the landscapes of John Piper and Paul Nash echoed so vividly the crisis of the Second World War reflecting a country under siege.

If one aspect of our identity is still to be found in the aesthetic of the pastoral and the rural, the other is epitomised by such words as empire, imperial and messianic. As Britannia, England had belonged to the Roman Empire but it never formed part of the medieval Holy Roman Empire. Yet from ancient times this mysterious island set on the fringes of the then-known world was haunted by an imperial vision. This was fed over the centuries by myth and legend and by the role of the English as the dominant people within the island. It was during the rule of Elizabeth I that the imperial vision was most powerfully expressed and became part of the national fabric of our country. It informed the Act of Union in 1707 and came to fruition in the creation of a global empire. It was to rise in a great crescendo in the eighteenth and nine-teenth centuries and then wither in the twentieth as the British Empire went into eclipse. Today Britannia no longer rules the waves – and with that we have yet to come to terms. The ghost of that past continues to haunt us every year in the Last Night of the Proms when we sing Elgar's 'Land of Hope and Glory', which hails the country as the 'mother of the free' and holds out the hope of an ever-expanding empire: that God who has made us 'mightier' would make us 'mightier yet'.

Who then are the English and what is England? I believe the answer to that question will only be found if we understand what constituted the shared vision and purpose of the country in earlier ages. This book takes the reader on a journey through history and mythology, art and literature, in search of the roots of our national identity. That identity rests firmly in the imagination and the key to the future lies in those icons and traditions that have retained their validity and still speak to us in the twenty-first century.

Prologue

England and the Imagination

The rural and the imperial vision.

PIETRO ANNIGONI'S PORTRAIT OF Elizabeth II in 1954 remains the iconic image of a period. Two years into her reign the young queen arises like a portent arrayed in her ceremonial robes. She is silhouetted against a serene but cold sky beneath which, receding into the far distance, stretches a misty English winter landscape from which leafless trees emerge to frame her. Annigoni places the sitter not before an urban panorama reflecting the reality of a modern industrialised nation but provides us instead with a poetic rural vision: England, as he saw it, was the countryside.

In that choice of a rural panorama Annigoni encapsulates a crucial aspect of the myth of England. But the figure of the queen and her costume, the robes of a fourteenth-century order of chivalry whose patron saint is St George and whose badge is the red cross that forms the national flag of England, spells another. This is a commanding, imperial image of a woman who was still the figurehead of a global empire that embraced the British Isles, Australia, Canada, New Zealand and parts of Africa. India had gained its independence seven years before but remained part of what was now reconfigured as the Commonwealth. In his portrait, Annigoni brings together the two threads which for centuries have composed the nation's identity – the rural and the imperial. More important still, it is through the imagination of artists such as Annigoni that these traditions continue to haunt us.

The queen's coronation had taken place in the summer of the previous year. In 1953 I was sixteen and in the sixth form of my grammar school in north London. Thanks to a county grant of £150 I was to go to Queen Mary College on the Mile End Road to read history. I was a clear beneficiary of the 1944 Education Act, which had only come into effect after the war, ensuring upward social mobility for a section of society which had up until then been denied access to advanced education.

In 1953 rationing was still in place, although the war had ended eight years earlier. There were glimmerings of a return to normal, although that was also to bring back the divisions of pre-war society. In the war years everyone had been reduced more or less to the same level; now, little by little, the complex class gradations reappeared, even in the lower-middle-class suburban street in which I grew up. I remember everything being unremittingly black, brown and grey in those years, until in 1951 the Festival of Britain presented a vibrant vision of the country which seemed to promise a glorious future.

I was taken to the festival by my mother and I recall not liking it. But by then I had fallen in love with history, portraits, pageantry and the theatre. And although I was unaware of it at the time, the festival was a triumph of the modernists – the planners and architects who created the new towns, demolished Victorian terraces and rehoused their luckless occupants in tower blocks. It is clear to me now that, like the much-reviled Millennium Dome in 2000, the Festival of Britain was in many ways an attempt to reconfigure a new national identity based in an imagined present.

My imagination, by contrast, was caught by the opulence of Cecil Beaton's stage sets evoking a world of aristocratic glamour before 1914 and Oliver Messel's visions of romantic fairy-tale grandeur in his sets for *The Sleeping Beauty* at Covent Garden, not to mention the prodigality of the New Look in fashion. By 1953 I was busy designing scenery and costumes for school plays, which may have been the reason why I was one of the two pupils chosen from my school to join local children on the Victoria Embankment to witness the great cavalcade. From where I stood, rather far back, I glimpsed little more than the top half of those who passed by. Like everyone else, I remember Queen Salote of Tonga waving bravely from her open carriage as the rain fell on her, and I do of course recall the momentary glimpse of the young queen and her consort peering out of the golden coronation coach, the diamonds in her tiara flashing even in the light of that dreary June day. The procession was seemingly endless and, although in hindsight it bore little relation to political reality, it seemed at the time to be the celebration of a great imperial power as the various contingents from the four corners of the globe marched by.

I arrived home in time to witness the ceremony in Westminster Abbey on a new addition to our household furnishings – the television set. And later that week, at a visit to the cinema, I saw it all over again but this time in glorious Technicolor and on a large screen. More than half the population watched the coronation on television; here a whole nation came together on the occasion of an ancient feudal ceremony over a thousand years old.

Neither Annigoni's portrait nor the coronation reflected the reality of the early 1950s; instead they represented an England of the imagination created by the power of art – whether on canvas or through spectacle. This is also true of virtually every other icon or tradition which we regard as 'typically English'. As I shall demonstrate, Constable's immortal paintings of his native East Bergholt in Suffolk do not record a reality but are a memento mori for a world destroyed by social and political change. Similarly, in Wordsworth's great poem about Tintern Abbey the monastery's ruins serve as a vehicle for a complex of emotions and personal reflections. We have to understand that what constitutes the identity of England is a selective kaleidoscope of such icons whose outward observation conceals an inner meaning. Here we witness the ennoblement of reality by art – which in turn has directly affected how we look at the reality it has immortalised.

But when did all of this begin? Where lie the origins of this huge and multifaceted phantasmagoria of images, words, music and rituals that make up the identity of England? I opened this book with a portrait of the present queen but perhaps, more truthfully, it should have begun with an image of her great namesake, Elizabeth I.

Chapter 1

Gloriana

ELIZABETH I HAS HAUNTED ME from the age of sixteen, when I became fascinated by her many portraits. That enthusiasm began in my first year of the sixth form when I took history as one of the three Advanced Level subjects and owed much to an inspiring teacher who had attended the seminars of the distinguished Elizabethan historian Sir John Neale, author of a classic biography of the queen. Postcards of portraits were purchased and carefully filed and any books in which I could find a new image of her were borrowed and copied. I had already made up my mind that I wanted to write a study of the queen's images and a degree in history would be a first step towards that goal. Some twelve years later, in 1963, my *Portraits of Queen Elizabeth I* would appear, by which time I was a young assistant keeper at the National Portrait Gallery.

Why did this period of English history have such a hypnotic hold over me in the early 1950s? The parallels with my own time were inescapable: the heroic story of the beleaguered isle which had defeated the might of Catholic Spain had recently been re-enacted in the war against Nazi Germany. And then, in 1952, a young woman ascended the throne as Elizabeth II.

I remember a cartoon published on her return from Africa to succeed her father, which showed the new queen stepping from the plane. Above her there was a celestial vision of the Virgin Queen passing to her the sceptre of state. But her successor would have none of it. In one of her earliest Christmas broadcasts the new queen specifically rejected any association of herself with her great predecessor. It was her good fortune, she said, to have been blessed with both a husband and a young family. No one could have foreseen how very different the fortunes of the two monarchs were to be, both presiding over unusually long reigns. Yet I vividly recall the optimism which, after the poverty-stricken war years, surged through the nation as the gorgeous pageantry of the coronation seemed to signal a new age of splendour.

If the 1950s vision of England is encapsulated in Annigoni's portrait of the young queen, the 'Ditchley Portrait' of Elizabeth Tudor is the iconic image of the nation's greatest age. Now dominating the gallery devoted to the Tudors in the National Portrait Gallery, the picture hung originally in the house of that name in Oxfordshire. It is, or better, was – it has been reduced in size on both sides – arguably the largest portrait of a single person to survive from the era. What we are presented with is a cosmic vision dominated by a life-size image of the queen standing in a silvery-white dress studded with jewels. A pink rose is pinned to her ruff and she wears a jewel in the form of a celestial sphere close to her left ear. The long pale fingers of her right hand hold a folding fan. To the left the sky is radiant

England personified.

with the new dawn she ushers in, while to the right behind her storms and lightning are banished by her very presence. The queen's feet are planted firmly on a map of England, its counties and rivers clearly delineated, set amid a sea heaving with voyaging ships and sea monsters. In this portrait the Virgin Queen *is* her realm – she is England personified.

The painting was commissioned by the queen's Master of the Armouries, Sir Henry Lee, early in the

1590s, probably for her visit to his country house at
Ditchley in 1592. It was Lee who inaugurated the annual
celebration of Elizabeth's accession to the throne on
17 November, whose chivalric spectacles contributed
much to the mythology of both the queen and her reign.
On that day, a tournament was staged at court to which
the public was admitted, special services by order of the
state were held in churches and bells pealed from every
parish church throughout the land. All of this was an
innovation. It reveals that in the queen's own lifetime
her rule was already popularly presented as a new
beginning, a new era in the country's history.

Interest in Elizabeth I has never flagged during my
lifetime. On the contrary, in recent years fascination
with the great queen has further increased with a seemingly insatiable public devouring yet more biographies,
films and television series that dramatise her life. This
public appetite isn't entirely surprising, for it was during
her reign that English identity was fully defined for the
very first time. As I will explore in this chapter, many
ingredients which we take for granted as the essence
of Englishness have their roots in the Elizabethan age.
Between about 1580 and 1610, during the reign of the
Virgin Queen and the early years of her successor, James
VI of Scotland and I of England, a great vernacular
literature came to fruition, a musical renaissance took
place, a theatre of global significance was created, the
country's religious sensibilities were framed, English
law was codified, the geographical confines of the realm

were charted and the seeds of a great maritime empire boldly sown.

All of this fell into place very quickly in a surprisingly short period of time. What are the reasons that explain the phenomenon? First of all, the victory over Spain meant that a Protestant regime which had started uncertainly three decades earlier had gained permanence. Between 1547 and 1558 the country had been ruled by three monarchs and undergone three religious and political revolutions which affected even the humblest country-dweller. The victory over the Spanish Armada in 1588 signalled the arrival of the so-called Elizabethan Settlement: England would remain a Protestant nation under Tudor rule. In addition, by the year of the Armada, most people in England had little or no memory of how things had been before the queen's ascent to the throne in 1558; they had only ever known the political and religious institutions of a Protestant nation. More important still, the challenges from both without and within – from Catholic Spain, the Pope, disaffected English Catholics and dissident Protestant factions – demanded a powerful political and cultural response which would define the new England. And much of what was created is still with us today.

This new configuration of the idea of England revolved around the person of the Virgin Queen. As we have seen, beneath her feet in the 'Ditchley Portrait' stretches a map of the realm over which she ruled in pretty shades of pink, blue, green and yellow, each colour delineating a county. When she had come to the throne such a depiction would barely have been possible: it was during her reign that the realm was mapped accurately for the first time.

As the Renaissance historian J. R. Hale has written, 'a man could not visualize the country to which he belonged' before the age of cartography. Thanks to the advent of printing and the new technique of engraving maps could be made accessible to a wider public in the Elizabethan age. This was a revolution made possible by the advance in methods of surveying which enabled man to place himself in his own physical environment – and provide evidence of his conquest of the natural world. Christopher Saxton's (1542/4–1610/11) *Atlas* (1574–9) was the first accurate survey of England, delineating the realm (including Wales) county by county with its rivers, ranges of hills and towns, although the few roads that existed are omitted. All of the maps bear the Royal Arms and the queen's patronage is manifest in the splendid portrait that acts as the book's frontispiece in which she sits enthroned between the figures of Geography and Astronomy.

Saxton was a Yorkshireman who had learned his craft from a surveying vicar, and in 1574 the queen granted him the manor of Grigston in Suffolk 'for certain good causes, grand charges and expenses lately had, and sustained, in the survey of divers parts of England'. This is the first mention of Saxton's involvement in surveying England and Wales, an enterprise undertaken under government auspices and with the financial backing of Thomas Seckford, one of the queen's Masters of Requests and Master of the Court of Wards. Saxton enjoyed royal patronage and was provided with a pass by the Privy Council that ensured he was given assistance wherever he went.

During the second half of the 1570s, Saxton's maps were published county by county, although sometimes two would share the same plate; in the end, there were thirty-four engraved plates in all and for the first time an Englishman could pinpoint exactly where he lived. In 1577, Elizabeth granted Saxton the exclusive right to publish his maps for a period of ten years. When he finally produced his *Large Map of England and Wales* in 1587, it was printed on no fewer than twenty sheets. It is some measure of Saxton's achievement that his maps were not displaced as the master geographical representations of England and Wales until the Ordnance Survey began the publication of 'one inch' maps in 1801.

We can catch the sense of fascination and pride which Saxton's delineation of England gave to his fellow countrymen in a set of geographical playing cards that were published in 1590 and incorporate his maps in simplified form. Each card depicts a county and comes with a descriptive couplet. About Wiltshire we learn that 'the people accompted warlike. / For Corne pasture and good woole, very plentifull', and Suffolk is described as 'a ritch and plesaunt countrey / Aboundinge in cheese and butter, and store of cloth'.

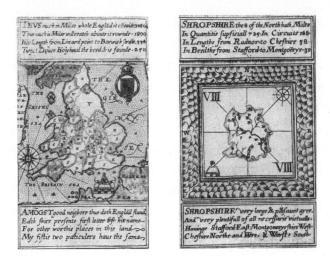

England mapped for the first time.

Through these maps England was for the first time visually defined. John Speed's (1551/2–1629) county maps in his *Theatre of the Empire of Great Britaine*, published in 1611–12, seven years into the reign of Elizabeth's successor, King James I, drew heavily on Saxton's but often added boundaries and roads. Speed belonged to a circle that included members of the original Elizabethan Society of Antiquaries, such as the historian William Camden (1551–1623) and the manuscript collector Sir Robert Cotton (1571–1631), and which reflected the late Elizabethan and Jacobean interest in English history and the country's historic buildings and monuments. In an innovative move, Speed associated the nation's landscape with its past. The map of Lancaster, for example, not only showed an inset plan of the county palatine but portraits of members of the rival houses of York and Lancaster who had fought the Wars of the Roses; that of Cambridgeshire included a map of the university city, depicted academic worthies in their robes and showed the arms of the university's many colleges. The physical presence and identity of the country are interlocked with its past. In that Speed draws on a shared historical narrative, to which I shall return later.

But not only cartographers set out to map the realm. In his unfinished epic *Poly-Olbion, or, A chorographicall description of tracts, rivers, mountains, forests, and other parts . . . of Great Britaine* (1612–22), the poet Michael Drayton (1563–1631) described the cities, hills, vales and rivers of the counties of England and Wales along with their history. Here the English landscape becomes a mnemonic for the nation's history – a seminal move that would influence generations of poets. Drayton describes how he was driven to write his epic in reaction to those who 'had rather read the fantasies of foreign inventions, than to see the Rarities and History of their own Country delivered by a true native Muse'. The opening passage of the first book reveals a deep sense of pride in his native land:

> Of Albion's glorious Isle the wonders whilst
>   I write,
> The sundry varying soils, the pleasures
>   infinite . . .

What help shall I invoke to aid my Muse the
  while?
Thou Genius of the place (this most
  renowned Isle)
Which livedst long before the all-earth-
  drowning Flood,
Whilst yet the world did swarm with her
  Gigantic brood,
Go thou before me still my circling shores
  about,
And in this wand'ring maze help to conduct
  me out:
Direct my course so right, as with thy hand
  to show
Which way thy Forests range, which way
  thy Rivers flow . . .

The books were illustrated with maps peopled with
allegorical figures, and the earlier volumes came with
lengthy commentaries by the great antiquary John
Selden (1584–1654), who annotated and expanded the
poet's historical and mythological references citing
original sources and chronicles. In this manner the kingdom's landscape and its history are inextricably linked.
In the words of Benjamin Disraeli: 'The grand theme
of this poet was his fatherland! The muse of Drayton
passes by every town and tower; each tells some tale of
ancient glory, or of some "worthy" who must never die.'

*   *   *

This cartographic discovery of England established a sense of the nation's boundaries, its identity in terms of physical space and the nature of the terrain. As we saw in the 'Ditchley Portrait', the newly found geographical knowledge also defined the political realm. More important still, this cartographic enterprise went hand in hand with a passionate interest in the nation's history, which was researched and rewritten to cast the queen's reign as the apogee of a grand historical narrative.

Chroniclers now began to abandon the medieval schema, which set historic time within the framework of divine revelation, in favour of the humanist model of the Renaissance that cast the past as a pageant of heroes and events, each of which carried a moral lesson for the present. The Tudor dynasty was swift to bring the nation's history into its orbit. Polydore Vergil's (*c.*1470–1555) *Anglica Historia*, published in 1534, presented the whole of English history as a prologue to the union of the rival houses of York and Lancaster in the marriage of the first Tudor, Henry VII, the victor over the Yorkist Richard III at the Battle of Bosworth, to Elizabeth of York in 1486.

The advent of printing meant that anyone who could read – or be read to – had access for the first time to the story of their own country. Thus the second half of the sixteenth century witnessed the birth of popular history writing. This began with Edward Hall's (1497–1547) chronicle, first published in 1548 and written significantly not in Latin but in the vernacular. Its full title gives us a good idea of its contents: *The Vnion of the two noble and illustre families of Lancastre and Yorke, beeyng long in continual discension for the croune of this noble realme, with all the actes done in bothe the tymes of the Princes, bothe of the one linage, & of the other, beginning at the tyme of King Henry the fowerth, the first aucther of this deuision, and so succesiuely proceeding to the reigne of the high and prudent Prince Kynge Henry the eight, the undubitate flower and very heire of both the said linages.* The title page of the 1550 edition shows a vast rose tree spiralling upwards, with its top branch revealing the figure of Henry VIII.

Two chroniclers virtually monopolised history writing in the Elizabethan age – John Stow (1524/5–1605) and Raphael Holinshed (*c.*1525–*c.*80). Stow was the more prolific of the two, whose chronicles, together with his famous *Survey of London* (1598), appeared in no fewer than twenty-one editions. His success reveals the enormous appetite Elizabethans had for an account of their own past – and that account in turn shaped their idea of the nation. What they learned is best gleaned from Holinshed's *Chronicles of England, Scotland and Ireland*, to the second edition of which Stow also contributed. It is an enormous work, the first edition of 1577 running to some 2,835 pages and the second appearing in 1587 in three massive volumes. This took the story of England to 1586 and was published at a time when patriotic feeling was reaching fever pitch, following the execution of Elizabeth's Catholic rival and claimant to the throne, Mary, Queen of Scots. Everything therefore is seen to lead up to the reign of the Virgin Queen:

> After all the stormie, tempestuous, blustering windie weather of Queene Marie was ouer-blowne, the darksome clouds, of discomfort dispersed, the palpable fogs and mists of most intolerable miserie consumed, and the dashing showers of persecution ouerpat: it pleased God to send England a calme and quiet season, a cleare and louelie sun shine, a quitest from former broiles, of a turbulent estate, and a worlde of blessings by good queene Elisabeth . . .

Holinshed freely embraced the myth and legend typical of the medieval chronicles, such as that by Geoffrey of Monmouth (*c.*1100–*c.*54) to whom we owe the myth of King Arthur, as much as historical fact. We can get a sense of this from some of the subheadings in the first book:

> Who inhabited this Iland before the coming of Brute: of Noah & his three sonnes, among whom the whole earth was diuided: and to which of their portions this Ile of Britaine befell.

> Of the giant Albion, of his comming into this Iland, diuers opinions why it was called Albion:

> why Albion and Bergion were slaine by
> Hercules: of Danaus and of his 50 daughters.

Working, like Hall, within a monarchical framework, the dramatic narrative reaches its climax in the
accession of the Tudors, who rescue the nation from
the turmoil of the Wars of the Roses. Holinshed's
account is patriotic and insular – any weakness in the
body politic is billed as some sinister pollution seeping
from across the Channel. This history of the nation as
the inviolate island was taken to the populace by
Shakespeare, who used Holinshed for his history plays
and for *Cymbeline*, *King Lear* and *Macbeth*. In a sense,
the history plays were the tabloid journalism of the day,
providing the largely illiterate masses with their past
in the sensational new format of the theatre.

Holinshed's *Chronicles* contained something else
reflective of the new-found patriotism – a wholly innovative attempt to define the English. This took the form
of the insertion, at its opening, of the cleric William
Harrison's (1534–93) *Description of England*. Working
from the premise that the English are a unique race,
Harrison writes:

> Such as are bred in this Iland are men for the
> most part of a good complexion, tall of stature,
> strong in bodie, white of colour, and thereto
> of great boldnesse and courage in the warres.

Harrison admits that the English are by nature slow-witted, yet this lies at the heart of a unique national characteristic – fair play:

> For it be a virtue to deale uprightlie with singlenesse of mind, sincerelie and plainlie, without anie such suspicious fetches in all our dealings, as they commonlie practise in their affaires, then are our countrimen to be accompted wise and virtuous.

On the other hand, Harrison admonishes his fellow countrymen for their passion for newfangled fashions: 'nothing is more constant in England than inconstancie of attire'. His *Description of England* was arguably the first attempt by an Englishman to define his own country and his fellow countrymen, and in the process Harrison covered a bewildering range of subjects: 'Of degrees of people in the Commonwealth of England', 'Of Cities and Towns in England', 'Of Gardens and Orchards', passing on to law and the universities, food and diet, buildings and furnishings, wildlife and the countryside – even remarking on dogs: 'There is no country that may (as I take it) compare with ours in number, excellency, and diversity of dogs.'

So far I have dwelled on the popular history writing which provided the Elizabethans with their past, but in terms of scholarship and lasting influence the most important work by far was William Camden's

The title page of William Camden's *Britannia.*

(1551–1623) *Britannia,* which appeared in 1586 and had gone through five expanded editions by 1607 before being translated from the Latin into English three years later. Camden's *Britannia* would have a far longer life than Holinshed's *Chronicles*: its last major edition was published as late as 1806. It has rightly been described by Wyman H. Herendeen as a work of 'the highest importance as a cultural icon affecting the national self-image'. Camden's aim was 'to restore Britain to Antiquity, and Antiquity to Britain'. Myth and legend, abundant in Holinshed, are jettisoned in favour of archaeological and topographical research that made use for the very first time of non-literary evidence such as coins, inscriptions and the physical evidence of the landscape: Camden only works from what he has seen and investigated with his own eyes. It was a revolution in history writing – in effect, it marks the invention of multidisciplinary history. Camden follows in Saxton's footsteps by describing in painstaking detail the landscape of England, monumentalising its topography and demonstrating how the events of the nation's history were etched into its soil.

These publications were the foundation stones that created a sense of national identity through an account of the island's physical topography and its history. To that we must add another key ingredient of insular identity – England's unique religious transformation.

Saxton's map of England recorded not only the nation's physical and political presence but also its ecclesiastical shape: the dioceses and parishes of what, after 1559, made up the Church of England. The break with the Catholic Church had been caused by Henry VIII's insistence that England was an imperial power over which no foreigner, such as the Pope, had any jurisdiction.

This view is enshrined in one of the defining documents of the Reformation, the 1533 Act in Restraint of Appeals to Rome, which opens with these famous lines:

> Where by divers sundry old authentic histories and chronicles it is manifestly declared and expressed that this realm of England is an empire, and so hath been accepted of the world, governed by one supreme head and king having the dignity and royal estate of the imperial crown of the same . . .

I will return to the theme of empire later on; at this juncture it is important to grasp that England became neither Lutheran nor Calvinist but opted for a religious compromise which reinforced national identity in a manner that was utterly unique in sixteenth-century Europe. The Protestant Church of England claimed not to be an innovation but a restoration to the purity of old before St Augustine was sent to these shores from Rome at the close of the sixth century. England's ecclesiastical identity too was locked into a remote past in the form of the Ancient British Church.

The new settlement called for theological explanation and foundation. The writings of three men were to define the Church of England in the Tudor period as it was to become familiar to the man in the pew for centuries to come: John Foxe, Richard Hooker and the Archbishop of Canterbury, Thomas Cranmer.

John Foxe's (1516/17–87) *Acts and Monuments*, which became instantly known as 'The Booke of Martyrs', was one of the most influential publications of the age. Its first edition appeared just five years into the new reign in 1563 and ran to 1,800 folio pages; in its later editions it extended to over 2,300 pages. While it is virtually unknown to modern audiences, its influence was to be enormous on generations of English people right into the Victorian age: it taught them an interpretation of the Protestant Reformation in which England was given a prime role in the cosmic struggle against the Antichrist, cast as the Pope.

For the anti-Catholic sentiments that followed the Reformation, the influence of Foxe's book can hardly be overestimated. The text of the first edition was enlivened by some 50 woodcuts, that of the second by 150. Together they provided dramatic and often lurid illustrations of the Protestant struggle against the Catholic Church in a manner which could only leave the strongest of impressions on readers. There they could see Pope Alexander III treading underfoot the Holy Roman Emperor, Frederick Barbarossa; the Emperor Henry IV with his wife and child waiting barefoot in the snow outside the castle at Canossa for an audience with Pope Gregory VII – both vivid examples of the popes' abuse of their spiritual power. Then there were the horrific images showing Protestant martyrs burned at the stake during the short reign of Elizabeth's predecessor, Queen Mary. In 1571, a copy of Foxe's book was to be placed,

Martyrs at the stake: woodcut from John Foxe's *Acts and Monuments*.

by order of Convocation, in every cathedral and it remained central to the English Protestant tradition, particularly through the seventeenth century. And there is no doubt that the book was widely read. I recall the person who taught me most, the polymathic Renaissance scholar Dame Frances Yates, telling me that, apart from the Bible, 'The Booke of Martyrs' was the only publication that she was permitted to read as a child on Sundays.

'The Booke of Martyrs' shows that even quite early in her rule, the accession of Elizabeth was presented as a seismic turning point – and these sentiments became stronger as her reign progressed. I have already mentioned the annual celebration of her Accession Day,

17 November, which began around 1570. This state festival helped to establish the myth that the Elizabethan age marked a new beginning – a *renovatio* of an ancient purity long lost. It is astonishing how the 'uniqueness' of the reign was affirmed, not in retrospect but by contemporaries living through it. Elizabeth's Accession Day continued to be celebrated through the seventeenth century, with festivities during which effigies of the Pope were ceremoniously burned, before it was taken over by 5 November to commemorate the Gunpowder Plot of 1605, when a group of Catholics tried to blow up king and Parliament. That is celebrated to this day – although its anti-Catholic intent is now glossed over.

The sixteenth century was a tumultuous age of religious revolution, often violent and bloody, as England first progressed from universal Catholicism to extreme reform, then briefly returned to the Catholic faith, before emerging as a Protestant nation, albeit in a unique form. The Reformation in England had been born of a dynastic crisis and right up until the 1580s there was still the possibility that Elizabeth could marry a Catholic – and had the forces of Catholic Spain landed and conquered the country in 1588 the whole history of England would have been different. Yet after the defeat of the Spanish Armada it was clear that the Church of England, with its own formulation of the Christian faith within the Protestant tradition, was here to stay. By then a new generation had come to maturity that had no memories of Catholic faith and ritual but had grown up with the words of the English Bible and the Prayer Book liturgy. And it was during those years that the Church of England was defined theologically by the great Anglican apologist, Richard Hooker (*c.*1554–1600).

The first four books of his *Laws of Ecclesiastical Polity* were published in 1593, and a further four volumes appeared between 1597 and 1662. By many historians this is regarded to be the first major work in theology, philosophy and political thought to be written in English, and Hooker is variously billed as the inventor of Anglicanism and a thinker whose work foreshadowed the Enlightenment. Hooker was the prime apologist for the Elizabethan religious settlement, which over the centuries would burgeon into the worldwide Anglican communion.

Throughout his work Hooker argued that the Church of England was a purged and reformed continuation of the medieval Catholic Church. More important still, and critical for the nation's fledgling national identity, he firmly believed that membership of state and Church should be coeval:

> We hold that . . . there is not any man of the church of England but the same man is a member of the commonwealth; nor any man a member of the commonwealth which is not also of the church of England.

In no other European country had such a radical solution been reached: to be English was to be a member of the Anglican Church – indeed, it became the *sine qua non* for anyone holding office in the governance of the state. It was a strong vehicle for national identity, which meant that first Catholic recusants and later, in the seventeenth century, dissenters were excluded from government employ and access to the universities. It was an ideological stance which was to last until the Victorian age, when these barriers against both Catholics and members of the dissenting churches were finally abolished.

Hooker's views echoed those of the queen. Elizabeth demanded outward conformity to the state Church, yet men and women could believe what they liked in private: she maintained that she did not want to open a window into men's souls. Hooker's Church of England was a visible community of worshippers who gathered in large and handsome churches. It was an institution with an established hierarchy of officers descending from arch-bishops to bishops, deans and archdeacons to rectors and vicars. In short, Hooker's Church reflected an ordered society stemming down from the monarch, who was its Supreme Governor, in which all worshipped in accord with the universal and immutable will of God.

And that worship was defined by the Book of Common Prayer. The Prayer Book had such an over-whelming effect on English religious sensibilities that it has to be given a central place in any consideration of national identity. Written in the incomparable prose of Henry VIII's Archbishop of Canterbury, Thomas

Cranmer (1489–1556), it had come in two versions. The first, more Catholic in outlook, appeared in 1549; the second, more reformist, in 1552. It was the second version that returned after the rule of Queen Mary, although Elizabeth was intent on muting its more strident tendencies. What set the Protestant services apart from the Catholic liturgy was that they were participatory: both minister and congregation played an active – and interactive – role in the liturgy, quite different from the medieval mass where the priest and worshippers acted almost independently of each other. The Prayer Book's language, constantly repeated Sunday after Sunday in the parish church, would soon become part of the intellectual make-up of the English people. In the words of the historian Eamon Duffy, 'Cranmer's sombrely magnificent prose, read week by week, entered and possessed their minds, and became the fabric of their prayer, the utterance of their most solemn and vulnerable moments.'

Until the second half of the twentieth century the English worshipped God with the words of the Prayer Book, made familiar and loved through endless repetition. They were also the words spoken in services that framed the major events in everyone's life – baptism, marriage and funeral. Here, as an example of its wonderful prose, are the words of the penitential prayer uttered by the congregation at morning and evening prayer:

> Almighty and most merciful Father; We have erred, and strayed from thy ways like lost

sheep. We have followed too much the devices of our own hearts. We have offended against thy holy laws. We have left undone those things which we ought to have done; And we have done those things we ought not to have done; And there is no health in us . . .

Such words shaped English identity for centuries until 2000, when the Prayer Book was replaced by *Common Worship*, which is now used in most churches.

Alongside the Prayer Book it was the Authorised Version of the Bible, commonly referred to as the King James Bible, which shaped Anglican worship. The fruit of a conference held by James I at Hampton Court to reconcile the Puritans to the rites of the Church of England, it was published in 1611 and replaced the Bishops' Bible commissioned by Elizabeth. It quickly became the only vernacular version of the Scriptures and would be familiar to every Englishman for over 350 years; to this day it remains unrivalled for its felicitous and inspiring prose. Many still know by heart the following passage, which is read every Christmas:

And it came to pass in those days that there went out a decree from Caesar Augustus, that all the world should be taxed . . . And all went to be taxed, every one into his own city. And Joseph also went up from Galilee, out of the city of Nazareth, into Judaea, unto the city of

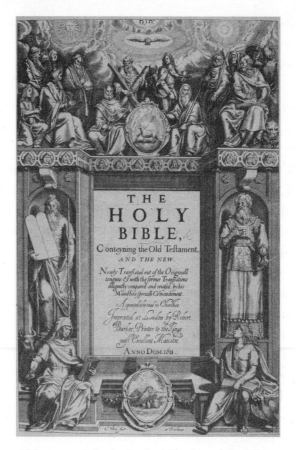

Title page of the Authorised Version of the Bible.

David, which is called Bethlehem (because he was of the house and lineage of David): to be taxed with Mary his espoused wife, being great with child. And so it was, that, while they were there, the days were accomplished that she should be delivered. And she brought forth her firstborn son, and wrapped him in swaddling clothes, and laid him in a manger; because there was no room for them in the inn.

Yet as in the case of the Prayer Book, more accurate translations, like the New English Bible, are now almost universally used in churches.

The Anglican settlement was unique in another way, for Elizabeth's determination to soften the more radical aspects of the Prayer Book gave birth to the English choral tradition. The queen's Injunctions of 1559 declared that

> for the comforting of such that delight in music, it may be permitted that in the beginning, or in the end of common prayers, either at morning or evening, there may be sung an hymn, or such like song, to the praise of Almighty God, in the best sort of melody and music that may be conveniently devised, having respect that the sentence of the hymn may be understood and perceived.

From Thomas Tallis (*c.*1505–85), William Byrd (*c.*1540/43–1623) and Orlando Gibbons (1585–1625) to Henry Purcell (1659–95), composers now set the words of the new Protestant services to music, resulting in a golden age of church music: Tallis's English anthems and settings of the canticles, for instance, are used in our cathedrals to this day. Without Elizabeth's intervention the great English choral tradition would not have come into existence.

The golden age of Anglican spiritual literature would still lie in the future, belonging to a generation only born during or after the queen's reign, such as John Donne (1572–1621), George Herbert (1593–1633), Henry Vaughan (1622–95) and Thomas Traherne (*c.*1636–74). But they could draw on the triumph of the vernacular which established English as a great literary language during the closing decade of Elizabeth's reign.

In 1580, the great poet Edmund Spenser (*c.*1552–99) wrote to his friend, the scholar and writer Gabriel Harvey (*c.*1545–1630): 'Why a [*sic*] God's name may we not . . . have the kingdom of our own language?' It was Spenser's desire to make the English language the equal of classical Greek and Latin: an astounding ambition as it called for works of literature to match Homer's *Odyssey*, Virgil's *Aeneid* and Ovid's *Metamorphoses*. Yet this is precisely what was achieved at the close of the sixteenth century with the appearance of a succession of literary masterpieces.

The foundation stone for this flowering of the English language had been laid two centuries before with Geoffrey Chaucer (*c.*1342–1400), whose *Canterbury Tales* had been first printed by Caxton in 1475. Suddenly, in quick succession in the 1590s, came an outpouring of poetry: Sir Philip Sidney's (1554–86) sonnet sequence *Astrophil and Stella* (published 1591) and his pastoral chivalric romance, the *Arcadia* (1590); William Shakespeare's *Venus and Adonis* (1593) and *Lucrece* (1594, published 1609); Samuel Daniel's (1562–1619) sonnet sequence *Delia* (1592); Michael Drayton's *Idea, the Shepheards Garland* (1593); Henry Constable's (1562–1613) sonnet sequence *Diana* (1592); George Chapman's (*c*.1559–1634) *The Shadow of Night* (1594), *Ovid's Banquet of Sense* (1595) and a continuation of Marlowe's *Hero and Leander* (1598); Sir John Davies's (1569–1626) 'Orchestra Or a Poeme of Dauncing' (1596); and last but by no means least, Edmund Spenser's *Colin Clout's Come Home Again* (1595). These were rounded off with two extraordinary anthologies: *Englands Helicon* (1600) and Francis Davison's (*c*.1575–1619) *Poetical Rhapsody* (1602). English poetry had arrived.

But in terms of English national identity nothing was to rival Edmund Spenser's great unfinished national epic, *The Faerie Queene* (1590 and 1596). Wordsworth would hail Spenser in his own great poem, *The Prelude*, as 'that gentle bard, / Chosen by the Muses for their Page of State . . . I called him Brother, Englishman, and Friend!' Spenser's epic poem, the first three books of which were published in 1590, casts England as a 'Faerie Land'. It is dedicated to Elizabeth I and the queen herself appears in two guises, as Gloriana, 'a most royall Queene or Empresse', and Belphoebe, 'a most virtuous and bewtifull Lady'. The poem remained unfinished but in the letter to his friend Sir Walter Raleigh, with which he prefaces his work, Spenser explained that it was 'a

St George, the Red Cross
Night, in Edmund Spenser's
The Faerie Queene.

continued Allegory, or darke conceit' conceived around
the legendary figure of the young King Arthur. Its
purpose was 'to fashion a gentleman or noble person in
virtuous and gentle discipline', so each book is dedicated
to a particular virtue – holiness, temperance, chastity,
friendship, justice, courtesy and constancy – embodied
in the figure of a particular knight. The poem opens
with the Red Cross Knight representing holiness:

Upon a great adventure he was bond,
That greatest Gloriana to him gave,
(That greatest Glorious Queene of Faerie lond)
To winne him worshippe, and her grace to
      have,
Which of all earthly thinges he most did crave:

And ever as he rode his hart did earne
To prove his puissance in battell brave
Upon his foe, and his new force to learne,
Upon his foe, a Dragon horrible and stearne.

He is, of course, the future St George, 'faire ymp, sprong out from English race'. The patron saint of England had survived the Reformation and was assimilated into the new order of things. In Spenser's poem, which opens with a large woodcut of St George and the dragon, the saint, whose red cross standard presages victory, is cast as a symbol of what must be one of the earliest references to 'merry England':

For thou, emongst those Saints whom thou
    doest see,
Shalt be a Saint, and thine owne nations frend
And Patrone: thou *Sainte George* shalt called bee,
Saint George of mery *England*, the signe of
    victoree.

The poem evokes the mighty struggle of light against darkness, of virtue against vice and truth against falsehood, of the fledgling Church of England against the monster of Rome. The 'Faerie land' of England is bathed in a mystic glow and its queen hailed with words of a kind usually reserved for the worship of the Almighty:

. . . O Goddesse, heavenly bright!

Mirrour of grace and Majestie divine,
Great Ladie of the greatest Isle, whose light
Like Phoebus lampe throughout the world
    doth shine,
Shed thy faire beames into my feeble eyne,
And raise my thoughtes, too humble and too
    vile,
To thinke of that true glorious type of thine . . .

All the ancient mythology of the country, derived from Geoffrey of Monmouth's *History of the Kings of Britain*, found its way into the poem culminating in the magician Merlin's vision of the nation's future:

Thenceforth eternall union shall be made
Betweene the nations different afore,
And sacred Peace shall loveingly persuade
The warlike minds to learne her goodly lore,
And civile armes to exercise no more:
Then shall a royall Virgin raine, which shall
Stretch her white rod over the Belgicke shore . . .

Alongside this unprecedented poetic outpouring England witnessed what is arguably Europe's greatest theatrical renaissance since antiquity in the plays of Ben Jonson (1572–1637), Christopher Marlowe (1564–93), John Lyly (*c.*1554–1606) and, above all, the incomparable William Shakespeare (1564–1616).

As Jane Austen so memorably wrote in *Mansfield*

Title page of William Shakespeare's First Folio.

Park, 'Shakespeare one gets acquainted with without knowing how. It is part of an Englishman's constitution . . . one is intimate with him by instinct.' More than any other of the writers discussed in this chapter, Shakespeare contributed and still contributes to our sense of collective identity. He remains the touchstone of Englishness and never more so than in his history plays. In nine plays, nearly a third of his literary output, Shakespeare invested his creative talent in delineating onstage the nation's legendary and actual past. In the 1590s came the three parts of *Henry VI* (1591–2), *King John* (1595–7), *Richard II* (1595–6), the two parts of *Henry IV* and *Richard III* (*c.*1596 and *c.*1592–4), and *Henry V* (1599). Later, in the reign of James I, followed *King Lear* (1605–6) and *Henry VIII* (1613). These put onstage for the London populace the Tudor myth as recorded by Holinshed and in such powerful form that over four centuries later the stories they tell still have greater potency over the imagination than the truths unearthed by modern historians; no one has ever quite been able, for instance, to whitewash Richard III of his crimes.

The plays present Renaissance ideas about political morality, concepts of kingship and the nature of the family and the state, as well as warnings about the dire consequences of rebellion, enquiries into divine providence and lengthy treatises on the Tudor myth. Although they were hugely complex panoramas of the past, they offered the contemporary audience an interpretation which enabled them to locate themselves in the present. Like the work of the Elizabethan cartographers, these plays mapped the nation's history and destiny, revealing the audience's place within it.

The plays also taught theatregoers the horrors that awaited any state in which the natural God-ordained hierarchical order was disrupted. Reaching a far wider audience than the printed chronicles of Stow and Holinshed, which were accessible only to a literary elite

– after all, anyone who could pay was allowed into the wooden O – those who came to see the plays were reminded time and again that they lived in a special age: an era of stability, felicity, certainty and cohesiveness as a result of their own queen's long reign.

Throughout his works Shakespeare refers to England 247 times and to the English 143 times, the vast majority occurring in the history plays; in *Henry V* England is mentioned on 49 occasions. Yet the speech that was to echo down the centuries as a touchstone of the country's identity is the dying John of Gaunt's elegy in *Richard II*: a lamentation for the passing of an England which – ironically, as historians now agree – was in fact being defined during that period for the first time:

> This royal throne of kings, this scepter'd
>   isle,
> This earth of majesty, this seat of Mars,
> This other Eden, demi-paradise,
> This fortress built by Nature for herself
> Against infection and the hand of war,
> This happy breed of men, this little world,
> This precious stone set in the silver sea,
> Which serves it in the office of a wall
> Or as a moat defensive to a house,
> Against the envy of less happier lands,
> This blessed plot, this earth, this realm, this
>   England,

> This nurse, this teeming womb of royal
>   kings,
> Fear'd by their breed and famous by their
>   birth,
> Renowned for their deeds as far from home,
> For Christian service and true chivalry . . .

Here John of Gaunt mourns an England that has gone into eclipse, for Richard II 'hath made a shameful conquest of itself'. The island is cast in an almost apocalyptic series of images as a 'precious stone', 'a house', a 'fortress', a 'blessed plot', a 'throne of kings' and a 'little world' set apart whose rulers and people constitute a 'happy breed', both Christian and chivalrous. This is arguably the greatest vision of England in all our literature, which has resonated down the centuries to be quoted and given new meaning in the face of any threats from without. It also inextricably links the physicality of the nation – its description as 'earth' recurs twice – to its monarchy: England is a 'scepter'd isle', 'the earth of majesty' and a 'teeming womb of royal kings'. The speech could almost be read as the literary equivalent of the 'Ditchley Portrait'.

Shakespeare remains the greatest monument to what, through subsequent centuries, became universally recognised as the golden age of literature. But in the context of this book he is much more than that. Through his plays the Elizabethan age and its vision of England are perpetually reborn for successive generations.

*　*　*

Yet the spheres of cultural endeavour – cartography, history, literature and drama – were not the only ones to ferment a national identity at the close of the sixteenth century. Elizabeth was also to preside over two other crucial and defining developments – the first structuring political life in the realm, the second laying the foundation of a future global empire.

When Elizabeth came to the throne English common law was unwritten and in a vulnerable state of disarray. On the Continent, Roman law, as epitomised in the Emperor Justinian's (527–65) *Corpus Juris Civilis*, was a written body and the province of professors. In sharp contrast, English law was administered by serjeants-at-law, based on precedent and recorded not in Latin but in legal French. And unlike the Continent, in England the monarch had no power to alter the law without the assent of the whole realm as represented by Parliament. This was fundamental to our native liberties.

Under Elizabeth and James I there occurred a national consolidation of law in written form, a process already begun in the fifteenth century with a series of works on the English government and constitution by Sir John Fortescue (1394–1476), whose *De Laudibus Legum Angliae* (1470) asserted the advantages of English common law over the Roman law of the Continent. The consolidation was almost entirely the work of one man, Sir Edward Coke (1552–1634), of whom his contemporaries said that he would be celebrated 'whilst Fame hath a trumpet left her, and any breath to blow therein'. His most famous pronouncement has passed into common parlance: 'An Englishman's home is his castle.' The great legal historian Sir William Holdsworth (1871–1944), in his magisterial history of English law, wrote that Coke's works were to the common law what Shakespeare's were to literature and the King James Bible to the Church of England. Although Coke believed in legal French he also favoured the English vernacular, writing that 'Our English language is as copious and significant, and as able to express any thing in as few and as apt words, as any other native language . . .'

Coke was fiercely patriotic in his desire to trace the English legal system and constitution back into the mists of time. He argued that the unwritten law of England went back to the Druids, and upon Parliament he bestowed an ancestry reaching back to the Anglo-Saxons. He published a series of magisterial volumes – *Reports* (1600–15), the *Book of Entries* (1614) and the *Institutes of the Laws of England* (1628–44) – covering every aspect of the common law. He apotheosised Magna Carta as enshrining the rights enjoyed by all English people under the common law: for Coke the Great Charter of 1215 was the foundation stone of English liberties. The most famous of all its provisions can be found in Clause 39:

No Freeman shall be taken or imprisoned, or be disseised of his Freehold, or Liberties, or free Customs, or be outlawed, or exiled, or any other wise destroyed; nor will We not pass upon him, nor condemn him, but by lawful judgment of his Peers, or by the Law of the land. We will sell to no man, we will not deny or defer to any man either Justice or Right.

Although the charter had been confirmed over forty times by successive medieval kings, by the middle of the fifteenth century it had ceased to occupy a seminal position in the country's political life. Its rehabilitation began in the Elizabethan period and was to play a major role in according the document the status it occupies to this day. England's unique legal system was to join the country's unique religious settlement in setting it apart from mainland Europe – and it explains why today the English feel uncomfortable with the laws passed by the European Parliament in Brussels.

In the 'Ditchley Portrait' the island kingdom on which the queen's feet rest is surrounded by waters through which ships plough their way in different directions. In the past, England's maritime power had been concerned with keeping the Channel free for war and trade with the Continent, but now these ships would venture further afield. With the reign of Elizabeth, the nation entered the era of exploration, discovery and colonisation. England looked westwards and would continue to do so in the centuries ahead.

This was the legendary period which saw the heroic voyages of Sir Francis Drake (1540–96), Sir John Hawkins (1532–95), Sir Martin Frobisher (*c.*1535–94), Sir Humphrey Gilbert (*c.*1537–83) and Sir Walter Raleigh (*c.*1552–1618). Their endeavours were chronicled by Richard Hakluyt (*c.*1552–1616), who recognised such maritime enterprise as a specifically English achievement in his *Principal navigations, voyages, traffiques and discoveries of the English nation, made by sea or overland, to the remote and farthest quarters of the earth.* Covering a period that ranged from the fourth century to the recent exploits of his countrymen, the book appeared in two editions: the first, running to 834 folio pages, was published in 1589, the year after the defeat of the Spanish Armada; the second, much enlarged, appeared in three volumes from 1598 to 1600.

Hakluyt wrote that he had been sustained in his task by his 'ardent love of my country', recognising the need

> to collect in orderly fashion the maritime records of our own countrymen, now lying scattered and neglected, and . . . bring them to the light of day in a worthy guise, to the end that posterity . . . may at last be inspired to seize the opportunity offered to them of playing a worthy part.

Principal navigations is a tale of maritime and commercial endeavour entwined, for not only did these adventurers set out to break the sea power of the king of Spain as it endangered the English market for cloth in the East and West Indies, but they were driven by the desire to seize the straits of Magellan and thence the gold mines of Peru. The enterprise was also motivated by the need to discover a north-east passage to 'cut Spain from the trade of the spicery, to the abating of her navy, her wealth, and high credit in the world'. Hakluyt tells the story of Drake's circumnavigation of the globe, the defeat of the Armada and the foundation of England's first New World colony, Virginia, named in the great queen's honour. Such enterprises cut across a broad spectrum of society, bringing together aristocracy, gentry and merchant classes, and we find their achievements vividly reflected in the pride felt in Drake's celebrated circumnavigation: in his engraved portraits the famed adventurer is always depicted with the globe of the world.

Hakluyt records an imperial and mercantilist vision founded on maritime power, which would find fulfilment in the creation of the British Empire. It also fuelled a tradition of voyages of discovery typified later by the likes of Captain James Cook (1728–79). Over the centuries England, which had begun under Saxton's auspices to map itself, was to map the known and unknown world. More important still, it was also to rule over a large part of it.

We have seen how the physical presence of England, its Church, its literature, its laws and its history defined

Elizabethan imperial
aspirations.

the vision of the nation as a sacred inviolable isle. But
the voyages of exploration that mapped the globe and
created the first colony point to another important idea
in the Elizabethan mind. If the 'Ditchley Portrait' depicts
Elizabeth's rule over the island, another famous portrait
of the queen portrays her as presiding over a world
empire. While we know that this vision became true
over the centuries, at the time it was an extraordinary
claim. The 'Armada Portrait' at Woburn Abbey depicts
Eliza Triumphans: we see the great queen in the aftermath of her mighty victory over Spain in 1588, which
is shown in the framed views in the background. The
most astonishing feature of the picture is that she rests
her right hand on a globe of the world seemingly laying

claim to it, an ambition that is confirmed by the imperial crown by her side. Other portraits of the queen depict her standing between the Columns of Hercules, the symbols of the boundaries of the Old World which also featured as the Holy Roman Emperor Charles V's personal emblem, signalling that her empire too would stretch to the ends of the earth. As we have seen, the legacy of this aspiration was very much alive in the 1950s and still lingers with us today. Where did this imperial vision stem from?

Between AD 43 and 410 'Britannia' had been part of the Roman Empire and those who claimed to rule the whole island never forgot that inheritance. In addition, according to legend the country had been founded by Brutus, grandson of the Trojan Aeneas, founder of the Roman Empire and hero of Virgil's *Aeneid*; the island was called Britain in his honour. In his *History of the Kings of Britain*, Geoffrey of Monmouth recounts the story and adds to it the figure of King Arthur, who was credited as the conqueror not only of Scotland and Ireland but of Iceland, Denmark and Gaul. Throughout the Middle Ages it was the English claim to rule over the whole island that kept alive the imperial idea.

The Tudors revived the imperial idea as the premise of their reform of the Church – 'this realm of England is an empire', the Act in Restraint of Appeals to Rome had declared in 1533. Spenser dedicated *The Faerie Queene* 'To the most high, mightie, and magnificent Empresse, renowned for pietie, virtue, and all gratious government,

Elizabeth, Queene of England, Fraunce, and Ireland, and of Virginia . . .', and in his *Midsummer Night's Dream* Shakespeare hails her as an 'imperial votaress'.

Yet despite this prevalence of the imperial ambition, the notion of a maritime empire emanating from what Hakluyt designated as 'the traffiques and discoveries of the English nation' was wholly new. And it was the invention of one man. In his *General and Rare Memorials Pertayning to the Perfect Arte of Navigation* (1577), the queen's astrologer and magus, John Dee (1527–1608/9), urged Elizabeth through her navy to 'enjoy, if not all our Ancient and due Appurtenances, to this Imperial Brytish Monarchy, Yet at the least, some such Notable Portion thereof'. As the descendants of King Arthur, the Tudors could lay claim to 'All those Septentrionall Iles, as BRYTANNICAS, which are in MARE BRYTANNICO'.

In his treatise *Mare Clausum* (written *c.*1619, published in 1635), the jurist John Selden (1584–1654) subsequently argued that the sea was 'capable of private Dominion or proprietie as well as Land'. Therefore, he concluded, 'the King of *Great Britain* is Lord of the Sea flowing about, as an inseparable and perpetual Appendant of the British Empire'. Dee, Selden and Camden all resurrected the figure of Britannia, which had first appeared on the reverse of Roman coins. She is personified as a female figure, wearing a helmet and dressed in classical robes, seated and resting her left arm, which embraces a tall stave, on a shield. She seems to sit on

Britannia implores Elizabeth to create the British empire.

ground that is rocky but Selden read the rocks as waves. As a symbol of maritime supremacy, Britannia was to have a long life on the nation's coinage but she was immortalised in this famous song from James Thomson's (1700–48) *Masque of Alfred* (1740):

> When Britain first at heaven's command,
> Arose from out the azure main,
> This was the charter of the land.
> And guardian angels sung this strain:
>
> 'Rule Britannia! Britannia rule the waves,
> Britons never, never, never shall be slaves'.

*   *   *

By the time of Elizabeth's death virtually all the ideas and images which together would form the nation's iconography for centuries were in place. By 1603 England had emerged as a tightly defined Protestant nation, the chosen 'peculiar' people of God, triumphant over the forces of Catholic Spain. During the Virgin Queen's reign, England had been mapped and described, her history written down and put onstage, her vernacular immortalised and her Church defined as both a reformed continuation of its medieval predecessor and a return to the purity of the Early Church. These were the foundations on which the nation was built over the next three centuries.

John Dee's invocation to Elizabeth that a mighty maritime empire be created through trade and colonisation was fulfilled by 1700 when thirteen colonies had been founded in America. The old imperial idea that the whole island should be ruled by one dynasty became reality when James VI of Scotland ascended the English throne as James I in 1603. And in 1707 the Act of Union with Scotland – followed by union with Ireland in 1801 – gave birth to Britain: an entity that was to be dominated by the English and in which the imperial vision that originated in the Elizabethan era would be played out.

Within the new configuration of Britain, the English initially avoided asserting their identity for fear of upsetting the equilibrium of an alliance that had produced a united island and ruled a vast global empire: to dwell on

England seemed irrelevant to a nation upon which the mantle of imperial Rome was seen to have fallen. Moreover, the English often referred to *England* when they patently meant *Britain*. Both the Welsh and the Scots clung on to their identity in the face of the English dominance within the union – but as long as England was dominant it never felt the need to define itself.

Yet England never wholly vanished. No sooner was the union achieved than it triggered a resurgence of 'Old England', largely in reaction to the dominance of French culture and triggered by the long wars with France in the eighteenth century. No one epitomises the revulsion at French style, taste and fashion more than William Hogarth (1697–1764), who in the 1730s emphatically signed one of his portraits 'W. Hogarth Anglus pinxt'. His series *Marriage à la mode* (1743) is littered with scurrilous attacks on the upper-class passion for Italian musicians and French dancing masters and hairdressers – foreign modes that were seen to corrupt the true values of Old England. Recording a visit to France in *O the Roast Beef of Old England* (1748), Hogarth assembled around the gate of Calais everything he disliked about the country as a land of 'poverty slavery and insolence'. At the centre of the painting a French cook buckles under the weight of a vast English sirloin steak, destined for an inn catering for English visitors, while a fat monk and starving French soldiers look on with longing.

The appearance of Dr Samuel Johnson's (1709–84)

William Hogarth's celebration of Old England.

dictionary of the English language in 1755 also reflected this resurgence of England. In the preface he wrote:

> I have devoted this book, the labour of years, to the honour of my country, that we may no longer yield the palm of philology, without a contest, to the nations of the continent. The chief glory of every people arises from its authours: whether I shall add any thing by my writings to the reputation of *English* literature, must be left to time . . .

More important still, it was during this period that there began a cult of medieval England and the

'England of Elizabeth'. This was fuelled by the rise of antiquarian studies epitomised by the re-establishment of the Society of Antiquaries in 1717, whose publications *Vetusta Monumenta* (from 1747) and *Archaeologia* (from 1770) began to make available the visual sources of medieval and Tudor England. In addition, a series of books published between 1773 and 1801 by Joseph Strutt (1749–1802) brought to life the splendour of Old England for the Romantic age, covering its manners, customs, dress, sports and pastimes. That reaching back to the English Middle Ages was deliberately cultivated by the Hanoverian monarchs, who had replaced the Stuarts but claimed descent from the country's medieval kings. Typical of this nostalgia, for instance, was Benjamin West's (1738–1820) series of paintings (1787–9) celebrating the deeds of Edward III, which was commissioned by George III (reigned 1760–1820) for the Audience Chamber at Windsor Castle.

This was of course also the heyday of the historical novel, which reached its apogee in the work of Sir Walter Scott (1771–1832), Harrison Ainsworth (1805–82), G. P. R. James (1799–1860) and Edward Bulwer-Lytton (1803–73). Last but not least, the revival of the Gothic style in architecture early in the nineteenth century recalled the era of Magna Carta, when the barons had subdued the arbitrary power of the Crown and secured native liberties. Gothic ruins sprang up in the newfangled landscape gardens as reminders of the nation's

The Victorian vision of Old England.

heroic past. It seemed inevitable, therefore, that the new Houses of Parliament, built in the aftermath of the fire of 1834, should be constructed in that style.

Thus the touchstones of English identity, many of which had originated in the Elizabethan era, continued to exist under the surface of the political union that formed Britain. But we are now well into the Victorian period when Old England flourished as a unifying factor in the aftermath of the Reform Act of 1832 and the extension of the franchise. What else did Elizabeth bequeath which framed the nation?

The Virgin Queen reigned for forty-five years. Under her rule England was rescued from roaring inflation and near-bankruptcy and provided with a religious settlement based on compromise, which ensured the country avoided the ferocious religious wars that would tear apart the Continent. Together with her greatest minister, William Cecil, Lord Burghley, Elizabeth gave the country wise government, working hand in hand with Parliament to bring political stability and economic prosperity to the nation. The evidence is still with us today in the black-and-white timber-framed houses of the age's prosperous merchants and yeoman farmers, and in the magnificence of the great houses of the aristocracy and gentry such as Hardwick Hall, Wollaton, Longleat and Hatfield. Elizabeth gave the country over three decades of internal peace, and the defeat of the Spanish Armada in 1588 marked the end of external threats. The result was a popular monarchy which, as we have traced throughout this chapter, rendered the queen a legend in her own time.

Moreover, Elizabeth will always be remembered for two of the greatest speeches ever made by an English monarch. Both are so important in any discussion of England and Englishness that they must be quoted here, however well known, for they lie at the heart of our

The island defended.

national identity. One was given in response to invasion from without by a foreign power, the other defined the queen's relationship with her own people. In subsequent centuries they were to become points of reference whenever England was under attack or a monarch abused his power.

The first was delivered to the queen's assembled troops at Tilbury on 8 August 1588, the eve of the Spanish Armada appearing in the English Channel. Elizabeth made her speech on horseback attired 'like some Amazonian empress' and holding in her hand the truncheon of the supreme commander of her forces:

> My loving people, we have been persuaded by some that are careful of our safety, to take heed how we commit ourselves to armed multitudes, for fear of treachery. But I assure you, I do not desire to live to distrust my faithful and loving

people. Let tyrants fear. I have always so behaved myself that, under God, I have placed my chiefest strength and safeguard in the loyal hearts and good will of my subjects; and therefore I am come amongst you, as you see, at this time, not for my recreation and disport, but being resolved, in the midst and heat of the battle, to live or die amongst you all, to lay down, for my God, and for my kingdom, and for my people, my honour and my blood, even in the dust. I know I have the body of a weak and feeble woman, but I have the heart and stomach of a king, and of a king of England too, and think foul scorn that Parma or Spain, or any prince of Europe should dare to invade the borders of my realm; to which, rather than any dishonour shall grow by me, I myself will take up arms, I myself will be your general, judge, and rewarder of every one of your virtues in the field. I know already, for your forwardness you have deserved rewards and crowns; and we do assure you, in the word of a prince, they shall be duly paid you.

Here the nation defines itself in defiance of invaders. External threat would be one of the key touchstones of national identity for the English – and after 1707 the British. It would come to the fore again in the mighty struggle against Napoleon, epitomised in Nelson's immortal line on the eve of the Battle of Trafalgar in September 1805: 'England expects every man will do his duty.' The queen's speech itself was famously echoed in Sir Winston Churchill's words to the House of Commons on 4 June 1940, following the evacuation of British forces from Dunkirk as continental Europe fell to the German armies and the nation was again under threat:

> I have myself full confidence that if all do their duty, if nothing is neglected, and if the best arrangements are made, as they are being made, we shall prove ourselves once again able to defend our island home, to ride out the storm of war, and to outlive the menace of tyranny, if necessary for years, if necessary alone . . . We shall go on to the end. We shall fight in France, we shall fight on the seas and oceans, we shall fight with growing confidence and growing strength in the air, we shall defend our island, whatever the cost may be, we shall fight on the beaches, we shall fight on the landing grounds, we shall fight in the fields and in the streets, we shall fight in the hills; we shall never surrender!

Elizabeth I's other great oration was given in peacetime. The famous Golden Speech, delivered to the Members of Parliament towards the end of her reign, defined the relationship of the English monarchy to its people. On 30 November 1601, some 140 MPs, with their Speaker, attended Whitehall Palace to hear the queen's final message to her people, delivered by the frail sixty-seven-year-old monarch – a remarkable age for the period – weighed down by her heavy velvet and ermine robes of state. Yet her magic touch did not fail her:

> Mr Speaker, we perceive your coming is to present thanks to us. Know I accept them with no less joy than your loves can have desire to offer such a present, and do more esteem it than any treasure of riches; for those we know how to prize, but loyalty, love, and thanks, I account them invaluable. And though God hath raised me high, yet this I account the glory of my crown, that I have reigned with your loves. This makes that I do not so much rejoice that God hath made me to be a Queen, as to be a Queen over so thankful a people, and to be the means under God to conserve you in safety and to preserve you from danger . . .

Her subjects had been kneeling in front of her and bidding them to rise Elizabeth closed her speech with these unforgettable words:

> It is not my desire to live or reign longer than my life and reign shall be for your good. And

though you have had, and may have, many
princes more mighty and wise sitting in this
seat, yet you never had, nor shall have, any
that will love you better.

The patriotism in evidence here is far removed from the
fervent nationalism of the nineteenth and twentieth
centuries. Yet the Elizabethan era has an intensity about
it which time cannot erode: what was created during
these years remains the rock of English identity. It was
immortalised within a decade of the queen's demise. Let
Shakespeare's *Henry VIII* have the last word on this
immortal period in our history:

> In her days every man shall eat in safety,
> Under his own vine, what he plants, and
>   sing
> The merry songs of peace to all his
>   neighbours.
> God shall be truly known, and those about
>   her
> From her shall read the perfect ways of
>   honour,
> And by those claim their greatness, not by
>   blood.

Chapter 2

This Blessed Plot

Every day I am made keenly aware that I live in England. Windows on the west facade of the house look to Wales. From the garden I can see the gaunt, barren silhouette of the Black Mountains, the range which geologically divides one part of this island from another and whose continuation is Offa's Dyke, that rampart raised up by a Saxon king in the eighth century to pen in the Welsh. On the other side lies what was, until the early fourteenth century, another country – a different terrain, bleaker and more vertiginous, yet with its own natural beauty. If I drive three miles to the brow of Saddlebow Hill I can look west into that alien landscape, but turning in the opposite direction I see laid out at my feet the golden land of my own county, Herefordshire, stretching east into the far distance towards Worcestershire, a panorama punctuated afar by the muted cadences of the Malvern Hills.

I live in a county that is composed of the same elements as every other: a city with a cathedral, seat of a diocese; a network of market towns; the great landed estates focusing on the country house (even if that is now often a school or a business centre and the land has long been sold off); a scattered patchwork of farms and farmland; and a web of villages each with its parish church. Such a framework, forged for the most part over a thousand years ago, is unchanging.

Yet each English county retains its distinctive regional character. Herefordshire is a poor but proud rural county, much fought over through the centuries, to which the castles that dot the Welsh border provide ample testament. This is marcher country, its land rugged and undulating, its soil an unforgettable tincture of red. The region's pride resides in its renowned breed of cattle and its orchards, in autumn hung thick with the cider apples which Lord Scudamore brought back from Normandy three centuries ago. To the north of the county one finds black-and-white timber-framed houses whereas in the south they are built of sandstone and brick. Many of its old families continue to reside here – the Cotterells at Garnons, the Hervey Bathursts at Eastnor Castle, the Clives at Whitfield and the Lucas Scudamores at Kentchurch. In spite of rapid social change there is still a strong sense of loyalty and continuity, of pride in the county and its history.

Herefordshire is one of those counties which seem to give substance to the image of England as the green and pleasant land that continues to haunt our imagination. Our fixation with the rural idea explains not only the creation of the National Trust but those endless battles over the erosion of the green belt, our resistance to the desecration of the countryside for new housing or motorways, and even our opposition to the felling of a single tree. What are the origins of our obsession with the countryside? Surprisingly perhaps, its roots lie not in reality but in the words of poets, in the vision conjured up by the painter's brush – and later by the photographer's camera – and the landscapes created by garden designers and plantsmen. All these impressions, with their separate histories, converged to create a landscape of the imagination – the rural vision of England. But to understand it fully we have to return to the Elizabethan period, where, as we have seen with so much else, it all began.

The roots of the rural vision lie in the literature of classical antiquity, in the poetry and prose of Virgil (70–19 BC), Ovid (43 BC–*c.*AD 17) and Theocritus (*c.*310–*c.*250 BC). These writers ignored the reality of the actual natural landscape in favour of an invented paradise, the *locus amoenus* which was defined by the great historian Ernst Curtius as 'a beautiful, shaded natural site'. To take just one example, here is an extract from Virgil's *Eclogues* (*c.*38 BC), which incidentally contains the first reference to the island of Britain:

> Ye mossy springs, and grass more soft than
>   sleep,
> And arbute green with thin shade sheltering
>   you,
> Ward off the solstice from my flock, for now
> Comes on the burning summer, now the
>   buds

Upon the limber vine-shoot 'gin to swell . . .
The junipers and prickly chestnuts stand,
And 'neath each tree lie strewn their several
    fruits,
Now the whole world is smiling . . .

It is in this guise of an Arcadian idyll that landscape entered England during the Renaissance, and when English writers of the Tudor period, such as the antiquary John Leland (*c.*1506–52), described their own country they resorted to the classicising form of the pastoral. Leland's description of Guy's Cliffe in Warwickshire owes far more to literary precedence than to any observation of reality:

Silence may be found there, a charming wood,
caves in the living rock, the happy sound of
the river rolling across the stones, little shady
groves, clear sparkling springs, meadows
strewn with flowers, moss-lined caves, ribbons
of water swiftly flowing between the boulders,
a solitary place as well, enjoying silence, which
of all things the muses love best.

Later in the century, Elizabethan writers, the creators of our national literature, transposed to England this idealised world of the poets of classical antiquity – and herein reside the origins of the English obsession with landscape and the countryside. In this pastoral vision England becomes Arcadia, an innocent sunshine world inhabited by shepherds playing their pipes, competing in eclogues and wooing their sylvan mistresses much in the same way as they do in Virgil's poetry. Man and nature are seen to be in perfect accord – and there appears to be no necessity to indulge in labour at all apart from rounding up the odd flock of sheep.

This Arcadia makes its literary debut in one of the great landmarks of English poetry, Edmund Spenser's *The Shepheardes Calender* (1579–80), a series of eclogues directly modelled on Virgil. Describing the lives of fictional shepherds, it not only discusses eternal themes like love and exile but also topical concerns such as the arrival of the new Protestant religion or the unreliability of court patronage. Inevitably, over it all the Virgin Queen presides:

> Contented I: then will I singe his laye
> Of fayre Elisa, Queene of shepheardes all . . .

In the accompanying wood engraving Elizabeth is shown holding a sceptre in one hand and an olive branch in the other, surrounded by music-making ladies in court dress. In the background a sun arises over a landscape in which shepherds play their musical instruments and tend their sheep. The great Elizabethan scholar E. K. Chambers perceptively wrote that 'It was possible, while preserving the main outlines of the pastoral convention, to bring it subtly into touch with English life;

Elizabethan England as Arcadia.

substituting the scenery, manners and customs, the legends and superstitions of our own countryside . . .' Elizabethan England began to colonise classical Arcadia.

Spenser dedicated *The Shepheardes Calender* to that flower of English chivalry, Sir Philip Sidney, whose most famous work, *The Countess of Pembroke's Arcadia* (published 1593), was to be read by every educated person well into the eighteenth century. Sidney too describes landscape in terms of the *locus amoenus* of antiquity:

There were hills which garnished their proud heights with stately trees; humble valleys whose base estate seemed comforted with refreshing of silver rivers; meadows enamelled with all sorts of eye-pleasing flowers; thickets, which, being lined with most pleasant shade,

were witnessed so to by the cheerful disposi-
tion of many well-tuned birds; each pasture
stored with sheep feeding with sober security,
while the pretty lambs with bleating oratory
craved the dams' comfort; here a shepherd's
boy piping as though he should never be old;
there a young shepherdess knitting and withal
singing, and it seemed that her voice comforted
her hands to work and her hands kept time to
her voice's music.

And, as in the case of *The Shepheardes Calender*, the scene
is peopled not only by pastoral folk but by figures the
contemporary reader would have immediately recognised. Here too Elizabeth appears, this time under the
guise of Queen Helen of Corinth, a woman whose 'beauty
hath won the prize from all women'. Sir Henry Lee, the
commissioner of the 'Ditchley Portrait', enters the tiltyard as Laelius, in chains and led by a nymph. Sidney
himself arrives as Philisides, the Shepherd Knight,
attended by squires attired as shepherds, their lances
disguised as sheep hooks. In fact, Sidney described with
some accuracy what took place in the tiltyard of
Whitehall Palace at the time: the fine line between
literary arcady and the reality of Elizabethan England
became progressively blurred.

Nowhere is this more evident than in the identifica-
tion of the queen's reign with the return of the golden
age. In Ovid's *Metamorphoses*, written before AD 8, this

had been the moment when Justice, personified as the Maiden Astraea or the zodiacal sign Virgo, descended from the heavens bringing with her perpetual spring-time and peace. Here is an extract from John Davies's *Hymnes to Astraea* (1599) written in Elizabeth's honour:

> E arth now is green, and heaven is blue
> L ively spring which makes all new
> J olly spring, doth enter;
> S weet young sunbeams do subdue
> A ngry, aged winter.
>
> B lasts are mild and seas are calm,
> E very meadow flows with balm,
> T he earth wears all her riches:
> H armonious birds sing such a psalm,
> A s ear and heart bewitches.
>
> R eserve, sweet spring, this nymph of ours
> E ternal garlands of thy flowers,
> G reen garlands never wasting;
> I n her shall last our state's fair spring,
> N ow and for ever flourishing,
> A s long as heaven is lasting.

Davies leaves no doubt as to the identity of Astraea: the verses form an acrostic, the opening letters spelling ELISABETHA REGINA.

This Arcadian tradition was to have a vast outpouring

A vision of England at peace in a Stuart court entertainment.

in poetry, painting and drama for over a century – much of it, it has to be said, derivative and repetitive. But even at that time, the rural dream it encapsulated was already dreamed by those living in an increasingly urban environment. It is a fantasy in which the country is seen as a place of content; where sorrow is banished and where it is possible to lead the good life; where true love flourishes and where simple manners stand in marked contrast to the studied artificiality of town and court. The country is a place of delight, of seemingly perpetual springtime with birdsong, where the ground is carpeted with flowers of every hue and season.

* * *

Thus the landscape of the Elizabethan age, the period during which England was defined for the first time, existed largely in the imagination as an idealised paradise: the people of Tudor and Stuart England still had to discover the reality of their own countryside. Even the word 'landscape' had yet to cross the Channel, first appearing in the text of a court masque written by Ben Jonson in 1605. That opened with a curtain on which was 'drawne a *Landtschap*, consisting of small woods, and here and there a void place fill'd with huntings'. This must have looked like a Flemish landscape painting of the period and is highly unlikely to have been a panorama of the English countryside.

Shortly afterwards, however, starting in the 1630s, a new tradition emerges that can be called the poetry of place. In his epic poem *Cooper's Hill*, begun in the late 1630s and completed just before the outbreak of the Civil War in 1642, Sir John Denham (1615–69) created a literary landscape. Whereas in the case of the pastoral the English were bidden to identify their native countryside with Arcadia, Denham asked them to survey an *actual* stretch of landscape as a series of mnemonics conjuring up the nation's past.

Standing on Cooper's Hill at Egham in Surrey, the poet looks down on the River Thames as it flows past Windsor and St Anne's Hill to the washland of Runnymede and Long Meadow and so to the metropolis. Windsor Castle is cast as an emblem of imperial greatness:

So Windsor, humble in itself, seems proud,
To be the base of that majestic load,
Than which no hill a nobler burden bears,
But Atlas only, that supports the spheres.

The castle speaks of peace and of the divine warrant of the English monarchy in the figure of Charles I, 'In whose heroic face I see the saint / Better expressed than in the liveliest paint . . .' The saint was of course St George, patron of the Order of the Garter whose seat was at Windsor.

St Anne's Hill to the east, topped by a ruined chapel that was once part of the monastery of Chertsey, speaks to the poet of the greed and dishonesty of the Reformation under Henry VIII. Contemplating the river, Denham meditates on the fertility which its waters brought to the agricultural lands that border it and the river's role in the country's industry and trade. The River Thames, temperate, regular and seemingly eternal, symbolises a well-regulated state and hence a well-harmonised kingdom.

Finally, the poet leads us to Runnymede, where, in 1215, King John had submitted to Magna Carta:

Here was that charter seal'd, wherein the Crown
All marks of arbitrary power lays down:
Tyrant and slave, those names of hate and fear,
The happier style of king and subject bear:
Happy, when both to the same centre move,
When kings give liberty, and subjects love.

Although Arcady lingers in the poem, Denham invites his readers to look very differently at the English landscape, and to read into it their own past and present. As a consequence, Denham's poem was to forge a long and powerful literary tradition – that of poems inspired by particular places often rich with historical associations upon which a poet ponders and meditates.

Alexander Pope (1688–1744) in his *Windsor Forest* (1713), published the year before the death of the last Stuart monarch, Queen Anne, also never quite abandons the Arcadian tradition. The hill on which Windsor Castle stands is cast as Olympus and into the surrounding forest strays Diana, the goddess of the hunt, who is pursued by Pan. But this poem too is rich in references to the country's medieval past – and its glorious future:

Not thus the land appear'd in ages past,
A dreary desert, and a gloomy waste,
To savage beasts and savage laws a prey,
And kings more furious and severe than they . . .
What wonder then, a beast or subject slain
Were equal crimes in a despotic reign?

Both forest and Thames proclaim the country's destiny:

Thou too, great father of the British floods!
With joyful pride survey'st our lofty woods;
Where tow'ring oaks their growing honours rear,
And future navies on thy shores appear.

The River Thames in particular seems to hold the country's destiny:

> The time shall come, when free as seas or
>   wind
> Unbounded Thames shall flow for all
>   mankind,
> Whole nations enter with each swelling tide,
> And seas but join the regions they divide;
> Earth's distant ends our glory shall behold,
> And the new world launch forth to seek the
>   old.

James Thomson's *The Seasons* (1726–30), arguably the most widely read pastoral poem of the eighteenth century, expanded the existing Arcadian tradition even further and adopted it to frame the new nation of Britain, which had come into existence barely twenty years before. In spring, Thomson writes:

> . . . the ramparts once
> Of iron war, in ancient barbarous times,
> When disunited Britain ever bled,
> Lost in eternal broil: ere yet she grew
> To this deep-laid indissoluble state,
> Where Wealth and Commerce lift their
>   golden heads;
> And o'er our labours, Liberty and Law,
> Impartial, watch; the wonder of a world.

There is still plenty of Arcadian bliss in Thomson's poem, where happy peasants work the soil in an idealised English landscape, but this tapestry frames an ever-expanding panorama of imperial greatness. That is well caught in the following scene taking place after sheep-shearing in summer:

> A simple scene! Yet hence Britannia sees
> Her solid grandeur rise: hence she
>   commands
> Th'exalted stores of every brighter clime,
> The treasures of the Sun without his rage:
> Hence, fervent all, with culture, toil, and
>   arts,
> Wide glows her land: her dreadful thunder
>   hence
> Rides o'er the waves sublime, and now, ev'n
>   now,
> Impending hangs o'er Gallia's humbled
>   coast;
> Hence rules the circling deep, and awes the
>   world.

Here the classical references are of a different kind: for Thomson, the nation's mercantilist and imperialist ambitions turn Britons into the inheritors of the heroes of imperial Rome.

With Thomson's *Seasons* we are within reach of the Industrial Revolution, which would soon transform the country. It is ironic that the countryside consolidated its position as an icon of the nation's identity at precisely the moment when England became the first country in the world to undergo industrialisation. To understand why that happened we must look beyond the literary tradition to another powerful art form which had an even greater hold on the English imagination.

In the last chapter, the physicality of the land entered our story in the context of cartography. We now need to look at it in terms of ownership. In England, land-owning represented economic wealth, social status and political power, as it brought the vote or even the control of a seat in Parliament. There was a widespread belief that civic virtue – that is, a disinterested concern for the country – depended on landownership, with the estate being seen as the nation in microcosm. Although that position would be progressively eroded due to the rise of the professional classes, land was never quite to lose its role as bestowing status in a society that was strictly hierarchical.

The young Thomas Gainsborough's (1727–88) portrait of Robert Andrews and his wife, Frances, is one of the masterpieces of English art. Painted in about 1750 the couple are arranged *en tableau* beneath a tree on their Essex estate. They had been married in 1748 when he was twenty-three and she only sixteen; this may have been a love match but was more likely to have been the coming together of two landed estates. The

Status bestowed by landownership.

painting is that rare instance when an artist of that period portrayed an actual landscape, for art historians have been able to locate the exact site and even identified the tree. The fact that the sitters are placed to one side and that the rest of the canvas is taken up by a panorama of the surrounding countryside is some indication of the significance they attached to their estate. The viewer is asked to contemplate the abundance of the harvest in the stooks of corn; in the middle distance, flocks of sheep graze; yet there is no evidence of those who worked the land for them. The detail is such that we know that a seed drill was used to sow the corn, a recent agricultural innovation, and the sheep are firmly penned in to avoid any cross-breeding with a neighbour's inferior stock.

This presentation of the couple belongs to a genre that became popular in the eighteenth century: paintings of family groups in which the sitters pose on their estate, often with the house shown in the background. Arthur Devis (1712–87), for example, produced a beguiling succession of canvases of exactly this kind. Such a setting for a family portrait is uniquely English: it would have been unthinkable on the Continent. Unlike France, the established classes in England did not focus their existence on attendance at court. Here an absolute monarchy, as epitomised on the Continent by Louis XIV, did not exist: the English king was subject to the rule of Parliament. London was not visited because it housed the court but to attend Parliament when it was in session – or to marry off a daughter during the season. Nothing could be more telling than the uniquely English tradition of the country's elites being buried not in a grand metropolitan church but in the local parish church. The aristocracy and gentry's power base remained in the country, where magnificent houses attested to their wealth and power. But they were political monuments too: their elaborate suite of state rooms for the reception of the monarch shows that the king was expected to visit them rather than the reverse.

Thus it is not surprising that the country house became a key icon of English life. Ben Jonson's eulogy of Penshurst in Kent, the birthplace of Sir Philip Sidney and the seat of his brother, Robert Sidney, 1st Earl of Leicester, provided ample testimony to its important status. Written in the reign of James I, the poem was, like Denham's *Cooper's Hill*, to be the fount of a genre:

Thou art not, Penshurst, built to envious show
Of touch or marble; nor canst boast a row
Of polished pillars, or a roof of gold:
Thou hast no lantern whereof tales are told;
Or stair or courts; but standst an ancient pile,
And these grudged at, art reverenced the
    while.
Thou joy'st in better marks, of soil, of air,
Of wood, of water; therein thou art fair.

This is no sycophantic hymn of praise to some recently
built house but a eulogy to 'an ancient pile' devoid of
the ostentation bestowed by gilding and marble. The
poem celebrates the plenitude of the estate – its abundance of game 'to crown thy open table', its fish stocks,
orchard fruit and garden flowers – and lauds the hospi-
tality and piety of its owners. This is the estate as a
benevolent institution:

There's none, that dwell about them, wish
    them down;
But all come in, the farmer and the clown;
And no one empty-handed, to salute
Thy lord and lady, though they have no suit.
Some bring a capon, some a rural cake,
Some nuts, some apples; some that think
    they make
The better cheeses, bring them . . .

In this manner the country house begins a long journey – one which leads right up to Evelyn Waugh's (1903–66) *Brideshead Revisited* (1945) – not as an object of class repression (which it undoubtedly could be) but as a symbol of benign lordship.

Taking into account the centrality of the land in England's social and cultural history, it is not surprising that landscape painting should emerge as a genre in which the English were to be hugely innovative. Gainsborough's portrait of Mr and Mrs Andrews not only points to the importance of landownership but also marks a new departure: landscape painting began to abandon Arcadia for a rendering of the soil of England.

The poetic pastoral tradition had its equivalent in painting. At the same time that Gainsborough was recording the actuality of this Essex estate, John Wootton (1682–1764), who had recently returned from Rome, produced pastoral idylls inspired by the canvases of Gaspard Poussin (1615–75) and Claude Lorrain (1600–82), who were the undisputed masters of landscape painting at the time. Claude in particular was avidly collected by the English and conditioned what they considered a landscape to be: an elegantly balanced composition with greenish-brown foregrounds, a light green middle distance and a haze of blue beyond, the scene framed by feathery trees and suffused with an intense golden light.

In Gainsborough's painting, Robert Andrews

The reality of the English landscape recorded.

stands holding a gun and with a gun dog by his side, reminding us of the importance of field sports. Indeed, some of the earliest painterly records of what the English landscape actually looked like have come to us in the form of a specifically English genre – the sporting picture. Again, a single example will help us to get our bearings. James Seymour's (*c.*1702–52) *A Kill at Ashdown Park* (1743) is an early instance of this new art form. Here we encounter no longer imagined but observed topography, a wonderful panorama of the Berkshire Downs near Newbury. The painting records an incident in the sporting party of Lord Craven, whose house, Ashdown, is seen from afar and

ENGLAND PERSONIFIED
'The Ditchley Portrait' of Queen Elizabeth I
by Marcus Gheeraerts the Younger, *c.*1592

OWNING ENGLAND
Mr and Mrs Andrews by Thomas Gainsborough, *c.*1750

THE ENGLAND
OF THE IMAGINATION
The Hay Wain by
John Constable, 1821

ENGLAND UNDER SIEGE
Landscape of the vernal equinox
by Paul Nash, 1943

IMPERIAL AND RURAL ENGLAND
Queen Elizabeth II by Pietro Annigoni, 1954

whose parkland gates are glimpsed in the middle distance.

The newly fashionable fox hunting was to be virtually beatified by the brush of George Stubbs (1724–1806) in an unforgettable series of pictures of horses and men in a landscape. These too have no parallel in the European painting of the period. Unlike the invented landscapes of the pastoral idyll, Stubbs's canvases could incorporate, for instance, the countryside of Creswell Crags on the Nottinghamshire–Derbyshire border, showing two opposing ranges of high limestone cliffs, deeply fissured, irregularly shaped and overhung with trees and plants. In his painting of a grey hunter with a groom and a greyhound, dated 1762–4, Stubbs represented the sitter posed against the actual background of the Creswell Crags he owned. In this too we can detect a celebration of status and landownership.

Thus, in the 1760s, there began a debate as to whether English themes should be treated in a classical manner or presented in their own terms. Those who favoured the latter called for freedom from the perpetual shackles of the world of antiquity in favour of realism and contemporaneity; indeed, they regarded certain English scenes the equal of those of antiquity. Yet others responded by making England resemble the Italy of the classical ideal. The artist Richard Wilson (1713/14–82), in his *The Thames near Marble Hill, Twickenham* (*c*.1762), deliberately delineated the villas and landed estates along the river in a scene designed to equal the classical

England transformed into the Roman Campagna.

theme of *beatus ille*. By a sleight of the brush the 'happy man' in his rural retreat in Georgian England becomes the reincarnation of the Roman senator in his country villa in the Tuscan hills.

Wilson had trained in Italy and on his return to this country was adept at presenting an English country house, such as the home of the Earl of Pembroke at Wilton, as though it were some antique villa suffused with a golden Mediterranean light. That he did so fully accorded with the wishes of his aristocratic patrons for whom the Grand Tour was de rigueur until the outbreak of the long war with France in 1793. Throughout the eighteenth century, vast swathes of the educated classes visited Italy to study the ruins of classical antiquity and returned with a fervent desire to import that ancient heritage to this island. These were the people who would have purchased one of Wootton's classically inspired landscape paintings or responded to Wilson's ability to make their new Palladian mansion look as though it was set amid the landscape of the Roman Campagna.

During the first half of the eighteenth century, landscape painting, inspired by classical references, had appealed to the abstract ideals of the intellect. By the end of the century it was looked at in an entirely different way: a subject for contemplation had become an experience appealing first and foremost to the emotions. We now enter the age of sensibility when 'a man of feeling' was expected to show an affinity with the natural world. No other European portraits of the period placed their sitters so firmly within the realm of nature as those painted by Gainsborough and Joseph Wright of Derby (1734–97), which reflected this new cult of sensibility.

It is striking that this shift in responses to the natural world took place during the early decades of the Industrial and Agrarian Revolutions which were to obliterate or radically change so much of it. In the English imagination, the world of nature now formed an area in which man could enjoy privacy, freedom and contemplation away from the expanding industrial towns with their factories and smoke. In this way a new idealisation emerged that replaced the references to classical Arcadia: the English countryside begins to be cast as an enduring symbol of traditional values and the true relationships of a lost pre-industrial age. Yet while landscape was presented as an equalising element binding society together, the countryside began to change dramatically: mass enclosure and agricultural machinery produced the fields, hedges and clumps of trees which we see today and created an underclass of landless poverty-stricken labourers.

Thomas Gainsborough, the greatest landscape painter of the eighteenth century, is said to have constructed his landscapes in his studio using stones, twigs and other flotsam as the raw material for his visions of valleys with cattle drinking at ponds, wagoners beneath copses of feathery trees, church spires glimpsed amid summer foliage, and mountains soaring above distant dreamy landscapes. Here we witness this new idealisation of the English landscape – and a progressive retreat from reality. Gainsborough's early pictures, which pretty accurately depicted his native Suffolk, gave way to landscapes evoking an England refined through the painter's imagination into a realm inhabited harmoniously by both landowners and working people. These pictures reveal a sense of nostalgia for a way of rural life which had come under threat; they depict cottage scenes and cottagers whose poverty is all too apparent. Such paintings were hung on the walls of the very landowners who had transformed the countryside through enclosures and mechanisation but whose sensibility might move them to acts of sympathy and charity.

*   *   *

It took a long time for the English to look at their own landscape for what it was instead of imposing upon it the idealised pastoral vision of antiquity: the change really came when they began to travel around their country. By 1700 there were maps that gave routes, and better roads and better constructed coaches that progressively reduced the travelling time between the country's towns and cities. Travel was transformed from a slow journey undertaken out of necessity to an exploration that gave information and delight.

There is little sign as yet of enjoyment in the reports of the indefatigable traveller Celia Fiennes (1662–1741), who hardly passed a favourable comment on the landscape as she traversed the length and breadth of England at the close of the seventeenth century. Constantly complaining about bad roads and steep hills, she referred in passing to woods, parks and orchards, but her journals come to life only when she records with pleasure anything new that she encountered in a country house or town. One of the few occasions when she took delight in the English landscape was when, on a hill some six miles from Canterbury, she glimpsed the town from afar: 'so fine a sight of Canterbury . . . it being a very high hill commands the view of the Country a vast way, and such variety of woods rivers and inclosures and buildings that was very delicate and diverting . . .' In sharp contrast, the Lake District failed to make an impression and she kept losing sight of Windermere 'by reason of the great hills interposeing and so I continu'd up hill and down hill and that pretty steep even when I was in that they called the bottoms . . . I was walled on both sides by those inaccessible high rocky barren hills which hang over ones head in some places and appear very terrible . . .' Her journeys were made easier, however, by an Act of Parliament which allowed the erection of signposts and she is vehement in urging her compatriots to 'spend some tyme in Journeys to visit their native Land, and to be curious to inform themselves and make observations of the pleasant prospects, good buildings, different produces and manufactures of each place'.

Daniel Defoe (1660–1731) is Celia Fiennes's solitary successor, and his *Tour of the Whole Island of Great Britain* was published anonymously between 1724 and 1726. The prolific author of *Robinson Crusoe* and *Moll Flanders* never in fact visited all the places mentioned in the publication which took the form of a series of three letters that capture the country a decade on from the Act of Union of 1707. They are compendiums that, very much like Fiennes's journals, focus on commerce, industry and agriculture, and are interlaced with gossip and excursions into history. As a fanatical Protestant, Defoe gives old churches and cathedrals short shrift and often casts them as the lingering dregs of popery. Like Celia Fiennes, he comments on the state of the roads and on the difficulties of travel, especially in mountainous areas; but from time to time he does respond to the landscape. Here he is about to enter Dorset:

I have mention'd that this county is generally a vast continued body of high chalky hills, whose tops spread themselves into fruitful and pleasant downs and plains, upon which great flocks of sheep are fed. But the reader is desir'd to observe these hills and plains are most beautifully intersected, and cut thro' by the course of divers pleasant and profitable rivers, in the course, and near the banks, of which there always is a chain of fruitful meadows and rich pastures, and those interspers'd with innumerable pleasant towns, villages, and houses, and among them many of considerable magnitude, so that while you view the downs, and think the country wild and uninhabited yet when you come to descend you are surprised by the most pleasant and fertile county in England.

Celia Fiennes and Daniel Defoe were pioneers in their curiosity about England. But in the eighteenth century there emerged a section of society with time on their hands to travel – members of the merchant and professional classes, or the 'middling sort'. They formed what we call 'polite society': people who read magazines like the *Tatler* (1709–11) or the *Spectator* (1711–12 and 1714), who frequented the new coffee houses, visited spa towns such as Bath or Tunbridge Wells, went to the theatre and the opera, and attended the newfangled urban assembly rooms.

Everything changed when a parson from Hampshire told this new travelling readership not only what to look at but, for the first time, how to look at the native landscape. The Reverend William Gilpin (1724–1804) has been called the father of the picturesque. His response to the English landscape was influenced by the work of Edmund Burke (1729–97), whose *Philosophical Inquiry into the Origins of Our Ideas on the Sublime and the Beautiful* (1757) gave new significance to emotions such as awe and terror, according status also to darkness and solitude, silence and immensity of scale. Mountains, for example, which had been monstrous aberrations to Celia Fiennes, began to be appreciated for the first time. To the Burkeian responses Gilpin now added the picturesque. Any scene is picturesque, he wrote, if it forms a picture that is well composed and harmoniously coloured. The painter was to 'adapt such diminutive parts of nature's surfaces to his own eyes as comes within its scope' – in other words include what is picturesque and omit or alter inessential detail or unsuitable features. 'Trees,' Gilpin wrote, [the artist] 'may generally plant, or remove, at pleasure.' If a view would be enhanced by the introduction of an ancient weathered oak instead of the tree that is there in reality the artist should introduce it without scruple.

In this we encounter a new form of idealisation. The English landscape is edited in a manner akin to what can be achieved today through digitalised photography. The result was a painterly vision, although Gilpin admonishes the artist not to venture too much from fact to fantasy: 'He has no right, we allow, to add a magnificent castle – and impending rock – or river, to adorn his foreground.' But, on the other hand, if he wishes to introduce or omit a tree, for example, 'These trivial alterations may greatly add to the beauty of his composition; and yet they interfere not with the truth of the portrait.' There was a fine balance between truth and fiction and doubtless many erred on the side of the latter in their sketches of the picturesque views they had selected. What is more important, however, is that although the English are at last looking at the reality of their own countryside, they are being taught to 'edit' what they see.

Gilpin's landmark publication was *Observations on the River Wye, and several parts of South Wales* (1782), which triggered what was arguably the first boom in English tourism. Boatloads of visitors now sailed down the River Wye from Ross to Chepstow to relive the reverend's visual experiences: Gilpin was the man who taught the English how to look at their own landscape, albeit selectively, for the first time with admiring eyes. The boats were equipped with tables on which the tourists could draw each picturesque view as it appeared. To achieve this they came armed with what became known as a Claude glass, named after the French painter Claude Lorrain. This was a slightly convex mirror, four inches in diameter, which could be placed so it gathered one of Gilpin's picturesque tableaux into a tiny space

Capturing the beauty of
the English landscape with
a Claude glass.

producing both the colours and the detail in such a way
as to make it easy to translate them onto paper with a
brush. As Gilpin wrote, the glass would 'give the object
of nature a soft, mellow tinge like the colouring of that
Master'.

In his *Observations*, Gilpin taught such visitors how
to respond to the scenery. Goodrich Castle is 'correctly
picturesque': a sublime and noble pile soaring above the
afforested banks below which stretched a more tranquil
rural scene with cottages adding 'animation and interest
to the scenery'. Halfway to Monmouth, tourists could
admire Coldwell, an amphitheatre of towering cliffs and
'mouldering perpendicular rocks, which assumed the
most fantastic forms'. Finally there was Tintern Abbey,

'a very enchanted piece of ruin', weathered by the hand of Time with creeping ivy, moss and lichen adding to its beauty.

The discovery of England was greatly facilitated by the outbreak of war with France in 1793. The French Revolutionary and Napoleonic Wars were to last for over twenty years, which meant that a whole generation of English people were unable to travel on the Continent – a situation similar to that created by the two world wars in the twentieth century, to which I shall return later. Out of this isolation in the late eighteenth century came the discovery of England, Wales and Scotland. In the case of England it was to sanctify two tracts of the countryside – the Wye Valley and the Lake District.

Gilpin precipitated a steady stream of guidebooks. Thomas West's *Guide to the Lakes* (1778), which had gone through twelve editions by 1812, took visitors on a set route with fixed viewpoints in the Gilpin manner, rather like today's coach stops where tourists are bidden to step out and snap an obligatory panorama. Yet even now we still cherish the views described by West as quintessentially iconic views of England. Here is what he wrote on a dull autumn day as he approached Ullswater from Dunmallet:

> From hence I saw the lake opening directly at
> my feet, majestic in its calmness, clear and
> smooth as a blue mirror, with winding shores
> and low points of land covered with green

inclosures, white farm-houses looking out among the trees, and cattle feeding. The water is almost every where bordered with cultivated lands to a quarter of a mile in breadth, till they reach the feet of the mountains, which rise very rude and awful with their broken tops on either hand.

At the end of the eighteenth century this new view of landscape was intensified by Romanticism, which recast the role of the artist away from public man to someone who in his work enshrined a deeply personal way of looking at the world. To the Romantic artist what the inward eye perceived was more important than what the outward eye observed.

If we had to choose one painter who, above every other, embodied the essence of English landscape painting and at the same time took on this new role of the artist, it could only be John Constable (1776–1837). Today we tend to forget that his pictures were nothing short of revolutionary; indeed, he was only grudgingly admitted to the Royal Academy at the age of forty-three. The subject of almost all his paintings was the vicinity of East Bergholt in Suffolk and along the neighbouring valley of the Stour, which is today known as Constable Country. He explained his painterly vision in the famous letter to his friend, Archdeacon John Fisher:

I should paint my own places best – Painting is but another word for feeling. I associate my 'careless boyhood' to all that lies on the banks of the *Stour*. They made me a painter (& I am grateful) that is I had often thought of pictures of them before I had ever touched a pencil [brush], and your picture [*The White Horse*] is one of the strongest instances I can recollect of it.

Here the English landscape, rearranged but recognisable as a particular part of the country, reflects the painter's deepest thoughts and emotions.

The most iconic – and to me the most English – of all his pictures is *The Hay Wain*, exhibited at the Royal Academy in 1821 and now in the National Gallery. Constable's originality lies in the fact that he used landscape as a vehicle for autobiography – it becomes a reflection of himself, his family and their past. In the process, landscape was finally released from the burden of literary texts of classical antiquity and the pictorial assumptions of the old masters like Claude. At the time visitors to the Royal Academy would have been astounded by the enormous size of *The Hay Wain* – 130.5 x 185.5cm or 51¼ x 73 inches – for such a scale was normally reserved for scenes from classical mythology, national history or biblical stories. Instead they were presented with a view below Flatford Mill with a house anchoring the composition to the left. A horse-drawn

The supreme painterly icon of England.

hay wagon with a man and a boy aboard crosses the stream of water disgorged by the mill and turns to negotiate a passage across the main channel of the Stour. By the house a woman bends down to collect water, a dog scampers along the fore-shore and, just beyond the moored rowing boat to the right, an angler can be seen making his way through the reeds. In the middle distance we glimpse workers cutting hay and loading another wagon.

This painting is purely autobiographical. Flatford Mill had been Constable's father's first house and was where the painter's oldest sister and brother were born. It is thus a poetic revisitation of the painter's childhood, the result of sketching and looking at the same small area of country from every angle over decades before producing a summation, the fruit of a 'recollection in tranquillity'. But we must remember that what is immortalised here is not the present but a lost idyllic past. And to me this accounts for the hold of Constable's landscapes on the English imagination: living in the modern world we look back with nostalgia to a lost innocence caught in these poetic evocations of rural ordinariness. Although we can visit the site of this picture today, Constable's paintings depicted 'the dreams of a happy but unpropitious life'. All his compositions came out of the struggle to find ways of rendering his inner thoughts and emotions.

That Constable saw himself as an utterly English painter is evident from the epigraph in his *Various Subjects of Landscape, Characteristic of English Scenery* (1830–3), a collection of mezzotint prints of his oil paintings. Here he misquotes Wordsworth's 'Thanksgiving Ode', replacing 'Britain' with 'England':

O England! Dearer far than life is dear,
   If I forget thy prowess, never more
Be thy ungrateful son allowed to hear
   Thy green leaves rustle, or thy torrents
   roar!

The epigraph on the title page of the 1832 and 1833 editions is taken from Virgil's second *Georgic*:

Rura mihi et rigui placeant in vallibus amnes,
Flumina amem, sylvasque, inglorius.

Let my delight be the country; and the
    running streams and dells
May I love the waters and the woods,
    though fame be lost.

Here Constable seems to turn the classical landscape tradition on its head: Virgil's words, which had inspired many a classical Arcadian scene, are applied to his own work – leading him to admit that by choosing the countryside of his childhood as the subject of his paintings 'fame be lost'. In the long term fame was far from being lost, but in Constable's lifetime, landscape painting ranked as an inferior genre in the universally accepted academic canon, which accorded the greatest status to those who painted subjects from history.

The reading of one's own personal past into the landscape is of course also the subject of one of England's iconic poems, William Wordsworth's (1770–1850) 'Tintern Abbey' (1798) or, to give it its full title, 'Lines Composed a Few Miles Above Tintern Abbey, On Revisiting the Banks of the Wye During a Tour. July 13, 1798'. Like Constable's *The Hay Wain*, landscape here serves to look back at the past, with the poet recalling an earlier visit with his beloved sister, Dorothy:

> – Once again
> Do I behold these steep and lofty cliffs,
> That on a wild secluded scene impress
> Thoughts of more deep seclusion; and
>   connect
> The landscape with the quiet of the sky.
> The day is come when I again repose
> Here, under this dark sycamore, and view
> These plots of cottage-ground, these
>   orchard-tufts,
> Which at this season, with their unripe
>   fruits,
> Are clad in one green hue, and lose
>   themselves
> 'Mid groves and copses. Once again I see
> These hedge-rows, hardly hedge-rows, little
>   lines
> Of sportive wood run wild: these pastoral
>   farms,
> Green to the very door; and wreaths of
>   smoke
> Sent up, in silence, from among the trees!

This is English landscape as mnemonic, but of a kind far different from that of Sir John Denham or Alexander Pope. They had used landscape to explore the English past; Wordsworth uses Tintern Abbey not to dwell on the ravages of the Reformation, but in true Romantic vein to recall his beloved sister:

> Nor wilt thou then forget,
> That after many wanderings, many years
> Of absence, these steep woods and lofty
>   cliffs,
> And this green pastoral landscape, were to
>   me
> More dear, both for themselves and for thy
>   sake!

Yet while some artists imbued landscape with personal memory, others continued to find in it resonance of a shared national history. J. M. W. Turner's (1775–1851) landscapes could be rich with patriotic associations, even if the terrain was often bleak. In his series *Views of Sussex* (1820), the painting *Battle Abbey, the Spot Where Harold Fell* depicts the abbey with decaying trees caught at dusk; here a landscape view becomes a reminder of the Battle of Hastings and the death of the last Anglo-Saxon king. In Turner's *Harlech Castle, from Twgwyn Ferry, Summer's Evening Twilight*, exhibited at the Royal Academy in 1799, the castle with its medieval associations is seen from afar, a relic from an earlier internal war, while, in the foreground to the right, a ship is being built, reminding the viewer of the current struggle against France.

Victorian painters became obsessed with landscape. The Pre-Raphaelites in particular recorded the world of nature with an unrivalled intensity of observation – but again, just one example will have to suffice. William

England as Eden.

Holman Hunt's (1827–1910) *The Hireling Shepherd*, exhibited at the Royal Academy in 1852, depicts a young shepherd with his left arm around a village girl with a lamb on her lap. Scholars have emphasised the painting's symbolic meaning – representing the temptation and fall of Eve – but what is more remarkable is its realism, its veracity in recording an actual landscape: the meadows at Ewell in Surrey which Holman Hunt painstakingly recorded throughout 1851. Here the painter responded to the greatest critic of the age, John Ruskin (1819–1900), who had written in the first volume of his *Modern Painters* (1843): 'go to Nature . . . rejecting nothing, selecting nothing, and scorning nothing . . .'

Yet the most visionary painter of the age, whose work for me epitomises the England of the imagination, is Samuel Palmer (1805–81). During the period he spent at Shoreham in Kent in the 1820s, he created a dream-world of landscapes through which country people move as though engaged in some holy sacramental act. Palmer was heavily influenced by William Blake (1757–1827), who believed that the artist had the duty to purvey his unique personal vision. Thus Palmer wrote in 1825: 'the visions of the soul being perfect, are the only true standard by which nature must be tried'. He ennobled the English landscape with a spiritual dimension, producing extraordinary works which for later English artists, such as Paul Nash, John Piper and Eric Ravilious, reconciled the modern movement with the native tradition.

Palmer interpreted the English landscape with an originality and boldness of vision that was unprecedented before the mid-twentieth century. Take *The Valley Thick with Corn*, painted in 1825. Here a figure in Elizabethan dress reclines reading while the hills that envelop him are filled with an abundance that recalls the praise of God in a passage from Psalm 65, which the artist had originally inscribed on the mount: 'Thou crownest the year with Thy goodness: and Thy clouds drop fatness . . . Thy folds shall be full of sheep, the valleys also shall stand so thick with corn that they shall laugh and sing.' Palmer's haunting landscapes seem to give visual expression to his mentor William Blake's most well-known poem, 'Jerusalem':

England as a mystical paradise.

And did those feet in ancient time
Walk upon England's mountains green?
And was the holy Lamb of God
On England's pleasant pastures seen?

As early as 1784, the poet William Cowper (1731–1800) had written in his poem *The Task*: 'God made the country, and man made the town.' As the Industrial Revolution progressed, pride in the manufacturing achievements of the country began to recede as the squalor of the new urban configurations with their factories, slum dwellings, poverty and disease became evident. Cities and towns were no longer viewed with the interested enthusiasm of a Celia Fiennes or Daniel Defoe but seen as monuments to false ideals and sordid vulgarity. Artists and writers such as John Ruskin began to extol the life of the countryside as epitomising ancient stoic values and a social harmony which had been lost. The squalid reality of much of country life was glossed over as the rising professional classes succumbed to a new ideal, which ennobled country mansion and cottage, village and market town, and their embracing landscape.

In this we have arrived at the formulation of England and Englishness in the late Victorian era which created the dream image of timeless rurality that is still with us today. But by now readers might be wondering what happened to another icon of English national life – the garden. This will demand reconnoitring back in time but it will eventually take us back to the central thread and those crucial decades that witnessed the lasting reconfiguration of our national identity.

Few things tell you more about England than a train journey out of a major conurbation – a journey that affords an unfolding panorama of back gardens behind mile after mile of terraced or semi-detached houses. Some, of course, are little more than dumps, but most city-dwellers cherish that plot of land: they plant a patch of green grass and a flower border, and often include a fruit tree and a small patch for herbs and vegetables. There can also be glimpsed the tool shed, the compost heap and a paved area in which to sit and observe the seasons and the labour of one's hands. And that evokes a litany of events which are quintessentially English: the fruit and flower shows, the open garden days in towns and villages, and the flower and harvest festivals in cathedrals and country churches.

This phenomenon is a strong testament to the desire of those who migrated to the city following the Industrial Revolution to retain a link with the countryside. I recall my grandmother, who had grown up in rural Suffolk, peering at the plum tree in our back garden and pronouncing upon the crop. My father inherited that feeling for the earth, for planting things and watching them grow, often sitting quietly in the garden in the warmth of a summer's evening. It is from him that I must have inherited my green fingers.

Not long after we married, my late wife, the designer Julia Trevelyan Oman, and I purchased the house in Herefordshire with which I opened this chapter and embarked upon the creation of what many now regard as a major garden. In this we followed countless generations of urbanites seeking the timeless English ideal of the country house and garden. Over thirty years we laboured to transform a field into a paradise of clipped yew hedges, topiary, pleached limes, statuary, fruit trees, vegetables and flowers. It is a garden of rooms, of vistas, of ascents and descents, of mystery and surprise. It is also often not what it seems. Like Constable's paintings of East Bergholt, The Laskett is a personal mnemonic, where memories of friends and events in our lives are expressed through the art of horticulture: a sundial and 'Iceberg' roses recall the friendship of the photographer Sir Cecil Beaton (1904–80), a temple my directorship of the Victoria & Albert Museum, brilliant red poppies my parents-in-law.

The world still comes in pilgrimage to England as a horticultural shrine. In that we are blessed by being an island warmed by the currents of the Gulf Stream to the south and west. On the whole our climate is temperate, with mild, wet winters and cool summers being the norm, thus allowing a wide variety of plants to thrive, large numbers of which were brought to this land from all over the globe by travellers and explorers. Today a million acres of England are given over to gardening and no fewer than three thousand gardens open their gates to visitors on certain days each year to raise money for charity. Some five hundred are reguarly open to the public; the Laskett is one of them.

Gardening has always been regarded as a peculiarly English activity: indeed, it has assumed a key role in English identity. There are two main reasons for this. The first, as we have seen, is the weather. A Frenchman, the Abbé Le Blanc, wrote in 1745: 'It is to the fogs with which their island is nearly always covered that the English owe both the richness of their pastures and the melancholic spirit of their temperament.' André Mollet's (d.1655) *Le Jardin de plaisir* (1651) contains the first reference to the superior quality of the English grass and its potential for making parterres. Mollet had worked for Charles I and invented the *parterre à l'angloise,* made up of green turf cut into a symmetrical pattern. The well-kept verdant lawn remains an English garden icon to this day.

But there are also cultural reasons that explain why gardening became the favoured activity of the English. In 'The Garden', perhaps the most famous gardening poem ever written, Andrew Marvell (1621–78) claimed that it purged all the worries and woes of the world:

> Meanwhile the Mind, from pleasure less,
> Withdraws into its happiness:
> The Mind, that Ocean where each kind
> Does straight its own resemblance find;
> Yet it creates, transcending these,
> Far other Worlds, and other Seas;
> Annihilating all that's made
> To a green Thought in a green shade.

Gardens were seen as having curative powers for the English malady of melancholy. In his *Anatomy of Melancholy* (1621), Robert Burton (1577–1640) urges the melancholic to 'walk amongst orchards, gardens, bowers, mounts, and arbours, artificial wildernesses, green thickets, arches, groves, lawns, rivulets, fountains, and such-like pleasant places'. What Burton tells us is that English people, unlike their continental counterparts, for whom it was a place for parade and social intercourse, went into the garden for a very different purpose – contemplation.

I believe it was the Reformation which gave Englishmen their green fingers. In Catholic countries meditation took place in churches, monasteries and nunneries. In England the setting for contemplation became the garden. Denied the images that formed an important aspect of the Catholic faith as a result of the iconoclasm of the Reformation, the natural world instead became the medium for reflection. On Good Friday 1549, the reformer Hugh Latimer (*c.*1485–1555), preaching a sermon before King Edward VI and his court at Whitehall, had admonished his audience:

> Our Saviour Christ had a garden, but he had little pleasure in it. You have many goodly gardens: I would you would in the midst of them consider what agony our Saviour Christ suffered in his garden. A goodly meditation to have in your gardens!

There is a long tradition of Anglican horticulturalism in England. Gardening came to be considered as an appropriate occupation for a clergyman, as any reader of Parson Woodforde's (1740–1803) delightful diaries will recall: 'Busy all the morning in my garden, having enlarged my Pleasure Ground a Trifle taking in part of the small Field . . .'

The key to such clerical fascination with gardening can be found in John Laurence's (1668–1732) *Clergy-Man's Recreation: Shewing the Pleasure and Profit of the*

Art of Gardening (1714). Gardening, Laurence wrote, will make a cleric 'happy, by loving an innocent Diversion, suitable to a grave and contemplative Genius . . . Retirement I find therein, by Walking and Meditation, has help'd to set forward many useful Thoughts upon more Divine Subjects . . .' So gardening as a setting for godly contemplation crosses into the eighteenth century. But in a second book, *The Gentleman's Exercise*, published two years later, Laurence adds another important element: 'The exercise of a Garden and the entertainments of Contemplation, will appear still more desirable if one considers how difficult and dangerous a thing Conversation has now become, and indeed made so by the corrupt Passions and Humours of Mankind.'

The garden provided privacy and a hideaway from the troubles of the world. We must remember that the seventeenth century had been dominated by the religious divide in society, which would erupt in a bloody civil war. Afterwards, defeated royalists, like Sir Thomas Hanmer (1612–78), retired to their estates and cultivated their gardens. Aristocratic ladies, such as Mary Rich, Countess of Warwick (1624–78), paced their gardens in deep and holy contemplation. Such meditation is wonderfully described by the poet Henry Vaughan (1622–95):

> My God, when I walke in those groves,
> And leaves thy spirit doth still fan,
> I see in each shade that there growes
> An Angell talking with a man.

Gardening became a neutral ground that could be shared by all regardless of their religious or political opinions. Three hundred years later the garden is still an arena in which all conditions and classes of people can meet on an equal footing. It retains a uniquely English role for, in the words of John Laurence, 'everything that is innocent, safe, and entertaining . . . all the best and noblest Entertainments are to be met with in the garden'. All this is still expressed today in the many flower shows and radio and television programmes as well as magazines devoted to gardening.

In the eighteenth century, the English produced a garden style that was to circle the globe, crossing Western Europe and reaching the Russia of Catherine the Great. We still recognise it at a glance and refer to it as the landscape style; the French called it *le jardin anglais*. It too has its roots in landownership: it is the rearrangement of the parkland surrounding a country house to form a series of 'pictures'. Some of these would frame the view of the house from afar; others would focus on a small temple or other building in a grove. In its successive stylistic phases, running from the pioneering works of William Kent (*c*.1685–1748) to the picturesque phase of Humphry Repton (1752–1818), it could embrace hermitages, ruined castles, Chinese kiosks and pagodas; it could introduce new plant species and also change the terrain by creating lakes and waterfalls. The English landscape park, based on asymmetry and reflecting the diversity of the terrain, came to be seen as an expression of English liberties and constitutionalism – it epitomised man's creation of a natural world from which all the imperfections had been removed and the parkland arranged to accord with a painting à la Claude. Beneath the seeming chaos of nature lay order and uniformity which had to be 'helped', but in a manner far different from the stiff geometric style of *le style français*.

The roots of *le jardin anglais* lay in the previous century. The description of the Garden of Eden in John Milton's (1608–74) *Paradise Lost* (1667) was to assume the status of a prototype landscape garden with its serpentine lines, wooded theatres, natural treatment of water – and its rejection of 'nice Art / In Beds and curious knots':

> Thus was this place,
> A happy rural seat of various view;
> Groves whose rich Trees wept odorous
>   Gumms and Balme,
> Others whose fruit burnisht with Golden
>   Rinde
> Hung amiable, *Hesperian* Fables true,
> If true, here onely, and of delicious taste:
> Betwixt them Lawns, or level Downs, and
>   Flocks
> Grasing the tender herb, were interpos'd,
> Or palmie hillock, or the flourie lap
> Of some irriguous Valley spread her store . . .

God's garden was natural and irregular. As the diplomat Sir Henry Wotton (1568–1639) wrote in his *Elements of Architecture* (1624), as 'a fabric [i.e. a building] should be regular, so gardens should be irregular'.

Yet at a time when landscape painting began to free itself from the golden age pastoral of the painters, it was precisely those very pictures that were the fount of *le jardin anglais* in its opening phase. Their dreamy classical visions were to take on reality in many of the masterpieces of landscape gardening which we still visit with wonder today, such as Stowe, Rousham and Stourhead.

The principles of a new garden style are epitomised in Alexander Pope's celebrated verse epistle of 1731 to Lord Burlington (1694–1753), the founder of the Palladian movement in architecture, which rejected the prevalence of the baroque, and the creator of Chiswick House with its magnificent gardens:

> To build, to plant, whatever you intend,
> To rear the Column, or the Arch to bend,
> To swell the Terras, or to sink the Grot;
> In all let *Nature* never be forgot . . .
> Consult the *Genius* of the *Place* in all,
> That tells the Waters or to rise, or fall,
> Or helps th'ambitious Hill the Heav'ns to
>   scale,
> Or scoops in circling Theatres the Vale,
> Calls in the Country, catches opening Glades,

The English landscape garden.

Joins willing Woods, and varies Shades from
　　Shades,
Now breaks, or now directs, th'intending
　　Lines;
Paints as you plant, and as you work,
　　Designs.

Turning the garden into a series of carefully
composed pictures encountered on foot – and here Pope
makes explicit reference to painting – is a ground-
breaking and uniquely English development. Up until
then the focus had been on symmetry and pattern
designed and laid out to be looked down upon. The man

who pioneered the change was Lord Burlington's protégé, William Kent. As Horace Walpole (1717–97) wrote, it was Kent who 'leaped the fence and found all nature was a garden . . . The great principles on which he worked were perspective, and light and shade . . .' It was Kent who invented the ha-ha, that ditch which enabled an easy transition from the garden into the parkland and beyond. From these principles came a great succession of landscape gardens, the work of designers headed by 'Capability' Brown (1716–83) and Humphry Repton, of which some hundred survive to this day.

Like poetry and painting, landscape gardens too were vehicles for ideas and allusions, linking a surface to an inner reality. As a result, great sections of the English countryside were rearranged on a gigantic scale involving stupendous earthworks, the damming of streams to form lakes and rivulets, the transportation of fully grown trees and the deliberate creation of carriage rides and walks. Like the Reverend Gilpin's tour books, this was all designed to take the visitor on a set route along which he would glimpse a series of 'pictures' meant to evoke moods ranging from awe to patriotic fervour, from joy to love, from contemplation to mourning.

In no other country either has the garden been imported into the urban environment so forcefully, beginning in the eighteenth century with the creation of green squares in the towns and cities, forming a community garden for residents, to be succeeded by the municipal parks and tiny back gardens of the Victorian age, burgeoning at the opening of the twentieth century into another innovation, the garden city that gave birth to Hampstead, Letchworth and Welwyn. Suburban gardening was effectively invented by John Claudius Loudon (1783–1843), the prolific Victorian writer and father of the villa and town back garden. In *The Suburban Gardener and Villa Companion* (1838), he provided detailed instructions for laying out gardens as small as those which he categorised as fourth-rate, 'in which the house forms part of a street or row; and their extent may be from one perch to an acre'.

By then gardening had moved on from the picturesque of Repton to the High Victorian style which we can still see today in municipal planting, where brightly coloured annuals are grown in patterns en masse. It was to be at the close of Victoria's long reign, however, that there emerged a new and universally recognised English garden style that, with variations, was to have a vigorous life through the twentieth century. It consisted of the marriage of firm geometric structure with an abundant planting impinging ever so slightly over the purity of line which articulates it. That marriage stems above all from the alliance of the great architect Sir Edwin Lutyens (1869–1944) and the plantswoman Gertrude Jekyll (1843–1932), who together established a new form of painterly style, combining perennials by taking into consideration their form, colour, leaf shape and flowering

The archetypal English garden.

season in the herbaceous border. At the beginning of the twentieth century, Lutyens and Jekyll established the now classic progression from formality close to the house gradually giving way to shrubbery and woodland. As in the case of *le jardin anglais,* their garden style has been copied and emulated in the most unlikely places and climes around the world. And with them we have entered the era when England defined itself afresh and which will be the subject of the next chapter.

Gardens take us deep into the consciousness of the English – and indeed into the country's soul. Like the poets' vision of the English landscape that we encountered earlier, through the centuries the garden has

figured as an image of the nation itself. In the third act
of Shakespeare's *Richard II* two gardeners are overheard
bewailing that

> . . . our sea-walled garden, the whole land,
> Is full of weeds, her fairest flowers choked up,
> Her fruit-trees all unprun'd, her hedges ruin'd,
> Her knots disorder'd, and her wholesome herbs
> Swarming with caterpillars . . . ?

In the 1650s the poet Andrew Marvell, lamenting
the miseries of a disordered nation in the aftermath of
a bloody civil war, wrote in his poem 'Upon Appleton
House, to my Lord Fairfax':

> Oh thou, that dear and happy Isle
> The Garden of the World ere while,
> Thou *Paradise* of four Seas,
> Which *Heaven* planted us to please,
> But, to exclude the World, did guard
> With watry if not flaming Sword;
> What luckless Apple did we tast,
> To make us Mortal, and The Wast?

Over four centuries writers have framed their
ideal image of England as that of a well-tended garden,
in which the hedges are kept clipped and the flower
beds are weed-free, mirroring a well-ordered society.
Thus it is not surprising that for many the garden

came to symbolise the country. Rudyard Kipling (1865–1936) gave memorable expression to this potent image of nationhood in 'The Glory of the Garden':

> Our England is a garden that is full of
>   stately views,
> Of borders, beds and shrubberies and lawns
>   and avenues,
>
> With statues on the terraces and peacocks
>   strutting by;
> But the Glory of the Garden lies in more
>   than meets the eye . . .
>
> Our England is a garden, and such gardens
>   are not made
> By singing: – 'Oh, how beautiful!' and sitting
>   in the shade,
> While better men than we go out and start
>   their working lives
> At grubbing weeds from gravel-paths with
>   broken dinner-knives . . .

Written in 1911, this poem takes us to the heart of the second reconfiguration of our national identity to which we now turn our attention.

Chapter 3

The Rural Idyll

A COUPLE OF BOOKS STILL rest upon my shelves set apart from the others. There is a reason why I am so fond of them: they were presented to me as form prizes. The first, which I received for 1948–9, is *The English Castle* by Hugh Braun, with a foreword by Hilaire Belloc. The second, for 1949–50, is *The Cathedrals of England* by Harry Batsford and Charles Fry, with a foreword by Sir Hugh Walpole. Both were published by B. T. Batsford and the first editions had appeared in 1934 and 1936 respectively. Both were books that I had yearned to own at the ages of thirteen and fourteen and which I had borrowed from the local public library in Edmonton, where I walked three miles or so either way each Saturday morning. I can still recall the joy I felt when I received them and was able to put them on my own bookshelf.

These books revealed to me a world that I was longing to explore. St Albans Cathedral was the only historic building listed in them which I had actually visited, for it was within reach – by Green Line Bus – of the north London suburb in which I grew up. I was wholly unaware at the time that these titles were part of an outpouring of guidebooks on England, to which Batsford the publishers contributed substantially in the interwar years. My childhood and formative years at the grammar school, to which I went immediately after the war in 1946, were haunted by a country under siege, which I was unable to explore and could only learn about from books illustrated with black-and-white photographs. These books taught me that England's identity lay in her historic past, in the gentle rolling countryside, in ancient brick-and-stone manor houses nestling amid parkland, in villages where the houses gathered round the parish church whose tower dominated the terrain, a scene enlivened by a green, a pond and an inn. That rural idyll didn't strike me as particularly odd at the time: after all, my grandparents on both sides had come to London from the countryside in the middle of the nineteenth century, so the link with that world was still tangible. I was, of course, wholly unaware that I was drawn into a selective dreamworld, a construct of the imagination that bore little relationship to actuality.

The rural idyll had also been celebrated by wartime popular music which invaded our house during my early years, most famously with the following lines:

> There'll always be an England
> While there's a country lane,
> Wherever there's a cottage small
> Beside a field of grain.

Vera Lynn sang that 'There'll be bluebirds over the white cliffs of Dover' and there was Ivor Novello's 'We'll gather lilacs in the spring again / And walk together down an English lane . . . when you come home once more'. In reality the majority of soldiers would return to factory and office work and live in run-down Victorian housing or between-the-wars suburbia. But that did not dislodge the pastoral. In the previous chapter we have learned how the ideal of the English landscape was created by poets and painters – but how did this idealisation come to dominate the national imagination, and indeed shape our national identity?

There is no indication in this idyllic vision of England of the dreary smoke-begrimed realities of the Victorian cities, nor is there any hint that the countryside for most of the time was in the grips of an appalling depression. Yet it was a vision for which English soldiers fought in both world wars. This idyll contains little that is aggressive or chauvinistic; while it is of course patriotic, it is also peaceful, romantic and tranquil. Although seemingly secure in the present, it draws its strength from tradition and heritage. It was articulated during the late Victorian and Edwardian period. This was the second time that the English defined themselves; they have not successfully done so since.

Recent scholarship has demonstrated that this reconfiguration responded to the needs of the democratic age in an attempt to hold together a people at a time when Britain and her empire had already begun their slow decline. Although this vision drew heavily on the components of national identity which originated in the age of Elizabeth – the physical boundaries of the nation, the monarchy, religion and the law, language and history – it was, as we shall see, essentially defensive and inward-looking.

On the other hand, we must remember that within the union England was the dominant partner with a population at the turn of the century of some thirty-four million, five times that of Wales and Scotland combined. It was an era when the word England was shorthand for Britain. Thus the literatures of Scotland and Ireland were assimilated into 'English literature' and the island's history too was virtually equated with that of England: its other constituent parts were virtually written out of the narrative. Yet all of this could only work as long as the other parts of the island did not wish to assert their identity but acquiesced in playing a supporting role in what was in effect a Greater England. So while the rural vision was inward-looking and insular, it implicitly defined the English as the masters of the island.

During the final decades of the nineteenth century, Britain and her mighty empire began their slow decline in the face of the commercial, military and imperial ambitions of Germany and the United States. The major reformulation of English identity at that time did not mean a dramatic break with what had gone before; rather it consisted of a sharper definition of the country's traditions and values that were rearticulated in the face of universal suffrage and mass literacy. It is proof of the strength and flexibility of this reformulation that it saw the country through two world wars and, although now frequently under attack from academics and political modernisers, has not been dislodged from the minds of a vast swathe of the populace. Indeed, it is the England that still attracts millions of foreign visitors; it is a vision lodged firmly in the nation's past – and in the English countryside.

By that time the country was no longer the inviolable Protestant isle of Elizabethan times. For centuries England – and then Britain – had defined itself through war with France, but by the end of the Napoleonic Wars the old foe had finally been defeated. Moreover, with the passing of the Act of Emancipation in 1829, gradually Catholics and dissenters could be educated at the ancient universities and also hold government office. So Protestantism slowly ceased to be a uniting force in the island. The new identity that was being forged during the late Victorian period could no longer be based on war and religion. More important still, it had to be shared both by the old land-based ruling elites and the urban middle classes.

It is not surprising that it drew on the traditions we encountered in the last chapter: it was a vision rooted in a longing for the rural pre-industrial world. Writing in 1975, Raymond Williams (1921–88) pointed to the apparent paradox:

But so much of the past of the country, its feelings and its literature, was involved with rural experience and so many of its ideas on how to live well, from the style of the country house to the simplicity of the cottage, persisted and were even strengthened, that there is almost inverse proportion, in the twentieth century, between the relative importance of the working rural economy and the cultural import-ance of rural ideas.

While the Industrial Revolution had depopulated the countryside, with farm labourers migrating to the cities, in the second half of the nineteenth century it was to be colonised by the prosperous middle classes in search of the rural idyll. As revulsion against the urban squalor increased, the countryside was seen to embody the timeless essence of 'Old England', encap-sulated in the ancient manor house with its attendant village and parish church, which was enshrined in litera-ture and in the new medium of photography. Photographers like Henry Peach Robinson (1830–1901) portrayed rural life as seemingly unchanged: an England peopled by farmers, craftsmen and labourers pursuing their cyclical toil through the seasons.

This vision could draw on the poets of the Romantic movement, such as John Clare (1793–1864), whose verses described the Northamptonshire that he knew so well:

The new art of photography ennobles the rural idyll.

The even oer the meadow seems to stoop
More distant lessens the diminished spire
Mist in the hollows reaks and curdles up
Like fallen clouds that spread – and things retire
Less seen and less – the shepherd passes near
And little distant most grotesquely shades
As walking without legs – lost to his knees
As through the rawky creeping smoke he wades
Now half way up the arches disappear
And small the bits of sky that glimmer
    through
Then trees loose all but tops – I meet the
    fields

And now the indistinctness passes bye
The shepherd all his length is seen again
And further on the village meets the eye

The longing for the pre-industrial world that runs through the Victorian age is also captured by Matthew Arnold (1822–88) in his poem 'The Scholar-Gipsy', written in the 1840s:

O born in days when wits were fresh and clear,
    And life ran gaily as the sparkling Thames;
        Before this strange disease of modern life,
    With its sick hurry, its divided aims,
        Its heads o'ertax'd, its palsied hearts, was
            rife –

The great Victorian poets, Alfred Tennyson (1809–92), Algernon Charles Swinburne (1837–1909) and Robert Browning (1812–89), all immortalised rural England as a vehicle of their deepest thoughts and emotions. Browning, living in exile in Italy in the 1850s, contributed perhaps the most famous poem expressing a yearning for the English countryside, 'Home-Thoughts from Abroad':

O, to be in England
Now that April's there
And whoever wakes in England
Sees, some morning, unaware,
That the lowest boughs and the brushwood sheaf

Round the elm-tree bole are in tiny leaf,
While the chaffinch sings on the orchard bough
In England – now!

In the golden age of the novel, writers too invented a rural England and peopled it with a veracity that still haunts our imagination. Anthony Trollope (1815–82) had been assigned to reorganise the postal service in the south-west of England, a task that took over two years to complete and in the process of which he visited every manor house, vicarage, farm cottage and village shop in the West Country. The journeys were to bear fruit in his acclaimed series of novels located in the invented county of Barsetshire: *The Warden* (1855), *Barchester Towers* (1857), *Doctor Thorne* (1858), *Framley Parsonage* (1861) and *The Last Chronicle of Barset* (1867). At the opening of *Doctor Thorne*, Trollope described his imaginary county:

> There is a county in the west of England . . . very dear to those who know it well. Its green pastures, its waving wheat, its deep and shady and – let us add – dirty lanes, its paths and stiles, its tawny-coloured, well-built rural churches, its avenues of beeches, and frequent Tudor mansions, its constant county hunt, its social graces and general air of clanship that pervades it, has made it to its own inhabitants a favoured land of Goshen.

The mid-Victorian rural England which Trollope had encountered on his travels is here transformed by the literary imagination:

> I had it all in my mind – its roads and railroads, its towns and parishes, its members of Parliament, and the different hunts which rode over it. I knew all the great lords and their castles, the squires and their parks, the rectors and their churches.

Here a whole world sprang to life – one of villages with whimsical names such as Plumpstead Episcopi, Crabtree Canonicorum and Crabtree Parva, and great country houses like Ullathorne, the ancient seat of the Thorne family. And although this county reflected the reality of the rural England that Trollope knew so well, it is in accord with the work of the poets and painters we encountered in the previous chapter that the author chose to create an England of the imagination.

An even more powerful imaginary landscape is the Wessex created by Thomas Hardy (1840–1928), a province which the writer defined in 1912 as 'bounded on the north by the Thames, on the south by the English Channel, on the east by a line running from Hayling Island to Windsor, and on the west by the Cornish coast . . .' In Hardy's books Bath remains Bath but Dorchester is Casterbridge, Beaminster probably becomes Emminster, Bere Regis is Kingsbere, and so

The rural idyll as perpetuated by *Country Life*.

on. His novels are haunted by the power of the landscape, which is suffused by an ancient past. Nowhere is this more vividly caught than in the portrait of Egdon Heath at the opening of *The Return of the Native* (1878):

> To recline on a stump of thorn in the central valley of Egdon, between afternoon and night, as now, where the eye could reach nothing of the world outside the summits and shoulders of heathland which filled the whole circumference of its glance, and to know that everything around and underneath had been from prehistoric times as unaltered as the stars overhead,

gave ballast to the mind adrift on change, and
harassed by the irrepressible New. The great
inviolate place had an ancient permanence
which the sea cannot claim. Who can say of a
particular sea that it is old? Distilled by the
sun, kneaded by the moon, it is renewed in a
year, in a day, or in an hour. The sea changed,
the fields changed, the rivers, the villages, and
the people changed, yet Egdon remained . . .

Hardy catches something fundamental in the English
perception of their countryside: the primeval timeless-
ness of the landscape. Although the countryside has
gone through dramatic changes as settlements have
come and gone, as methods of husbandry have changed
and open strips of soil have become enclosed fields, the
landscape itself is timeless.

The late Victorian age brought the rural vision to
a new audience. It would find its most vivid expression
in the magazine *Country Life*, the first issue of which
appeared in the year of Queen Victoria's Diamond Jubilee
in 1897. There, week in and week out, city-dwellers who
aspired to life in the country could feast on images of
historic manor houses, gardens and villages, and learn
about rural sports and customs. Interiors were carefully
arranged for the camera in accordance with the aesthetic
promoted by the magazine. The fact that *Country Life* is
still in existence testifies to the longevity of the rural
idyll and its continuing appeal to those living in the cities.

As we have seen, this rural vision apotheosised the landscape of southern England: the old Anglo-Saxon kingdoms – Kent, Sussex, Wiltshire, Somerset, Hampshire and Dorset – with their cathedral cities, market towns and villages. It glossed over the inequalities of a rural society graduating downwards from squire to farmer to craftsman to labourer. It emphasised mutual obligation and respect and the time-honoured rustic virtues of honesty, decency, goodness and Christian stoicism.

During the first half of the twentieth century, this view of England spread out across the population. It triggered a huge outpouring of literature aimed at a middle-class audience, which from the 1920s increasingly ventured into the countryside by car. Publishers, which had hitherto catered for train travellers, supplied them with guidebooks to help them in their quest for England. Arthur Mee's (1875–1943) *King's England*, published from 1936, ran into forty-one volumes. The first volume of the *Shell Guides*, edited by the poet John Betjeman (1906–84) appeared in 1934 – Betjeman himself writing on Cornwall – and it is striking that these surveys of the nation's past were perfectly reconcilable with the avant-garde taste of the time, as is evident in the involvement of artists that included John and Paul Nash, Edward Bawden and John Piper. To the *Shell Guides*, which were published until the 1980s, we must add Nikolaus Pevsner's (1902–83) monumental *Buildings of*

Advertising the
rural idyll.

England, which began in 1951 and was completed,
forty-six volumes later, in 1974; in revised form it
continues to be issued to this day.

Travel writers too contributed to an ever-increasing
literature on England. H. V. Morton's (1892-1979) *In
Search of England* (1927) became a best-seller – a third
of a million copies had been sold by 1969, making it
one of the most widely read books from the interwar
years – and in *English Journey* (1934) the prolific J. B.
Priestley (1894–1984) published a far from idyllic record
of a country in recession with widespread unemployment

and poverty. Morton, on the other hand, endorsed the idealised countryside of the south – a patchwork of hedgerows, ploughed fields, sunken lanes, downland and thatched cottages – and apotheosised the English village:

> The village has no name. It is a village which many a townsman has seen in lonely foreign places, for it is the essence of England, the unit of all our social development, the germ of all that we have become, something almost too English to be true . . .

His was a quest for pre-industrial craftsmanship and rusticity, and he worked from a premise that remains essential in any definition of England: the country has to be searched for and we only catch occasional glimpses of its soul, such as when Morton writes: 'At night, especially under this witching moon, the streets of Shrewsbury take you back to Old England.'

Country writing began to emerge as a literary genre in its own right. W. H. Hudson (1841–1922) explored southern England in the opening decade of the century in a series of rural classics – *Hampshire Days* (1903), *Afoot in England* (1909) and *A Shepherd's Life* (1910) – describing the lives of ordinary country folk. The socialist George Sturt (1863–1927) similarly presented precise pictures of rural life in *Memoirs of a Surrey Labourer* (1907), *Change in the Village* (1912) and *The Wheelwright's Shop* (1923). Sturt does away with the

The timeless England of the mid-twentieth century.

rose-tinted spectacles and records a fast-vanishing rural world in which labourers are replaced by machines.

English life was recorded with extraordinary vigour at that time and its greatest visual expression is undoubtedly *Britain in Pictures* (1940–8), a remarkable series running to 126 volumes with a bevy of distinguished contributors ranging from Edith Sitwell (1887–1964) writing on women, Vita Sackville-West (1892–1962) on country houses, Cecil Beaton on photographers and George Orwell (1903–50) on the English people.

There was a renewed intensity to the idea of England during the war years when, once again, the island was cut off from the Continent; we must also remember that due to currency restrictions very few English people had the chance to travel abroad until the middle of the 1950s. Looking back in 1987, John Piper (1903–92), the artist who more than any other epitomised Englishness in the twentieth century, put these years into fascinating perspective:

> The change in England was precipitated by the war. Suddenly artists who had had constant inspiration and direction from Paris were cut off. No more exhibitions of Picasso or Braque, Miro or Giacometti, no more arguments in French cafes and studios. We were on our own. Then, all at once the object was thrust upon us. The fear of losing either the artists themselves or the precious buildings and sites of England inspired the establishment of the Recording Britain Scheme. Roots became something to be nurtured and clung to instead or destroyed. Objects we had not been able to look at, let alone see, because of their positive personality or the proliferation of other artists' visions of them, now became of great visual and emotional importance. Then the War Artists Advisory Committee was set up: not only churches and barns and castles, but,

engines, aeroplanes, factories, bomb damage, air-raid shelters and people were to be put down on paper or canvas. Because of these commissioned records, some artists at least, learnt to look at and see the point of things that they had totally discarded.

For me, this led to another exploration; the beauty-spots, rivers, mountains, waterfalls, gorges, ruins and cliffs, all visual natural dramas that we had been taught to shun by Roger Fry and Clive Bell.

Artists such as Piper, Paul Nash (1889–1946), Henry Moore (1898–1986), Graham Sutherland (1903–80), John Minton (1917–57) and John Craxton (1922–2009), and photographers such as Edwin Smith (1912–71), all began to create timeless images of England. Smith's photographs in particular, reproduced in books on English cottages and farmhouses, churches and gardens, became iconic and are unforgettable for their purity of vision. John Piper's rendering of the English countryside has a lyrical and, at times, tragic intensity, which makes him Constable's equivalent in the twentieth century.

It was inevitable that this tranquil rural vision would be used and manipulated by politicians. Initially it was colonised by the Tory Party, into whose creed of compromise, adaptation and continuity it neatly fitted, but tacitly it was soon adopted across the political

John Piper records the rural idyll under threat.

spectrum. In 1926, Prime Minister Stanley Baldwin famously addressed the Royal Society of St George with the following words:

> To me, England is the country, and the country is England. And when I ask myself what I mean by England, when I think of England when I am abroad, England comes to me through my various senses – through the ear, through the eye, and through certain imper-ishable scents . . . The sounds of England, the tinkle of the hammer on the anvil in the country smithy, the corncrake on a dewy

morning, the sound of the scythe against the whetstone, and the sight of a plough team coming over the brow of a hill . . . The wild anemones in the woods in April, the last load at night of hay being drawn down a lane as the twilight comes on . . . and above all, most subtle, most penetrating and most moving, the smell of wood smoke coming up in an autumn evening . . . These things strike down into the very depths of our nature . . . These are the things that make England.

Yet despite its use and abuse by politicians, the concept of England and Englishness that emerged in the decades after 1880 shaped the nation. It was based on the assumption that a country that is united in its ideals must share with pride a common language, literature and history. Although what these should consist of has been subject to debate, they remain the foundation stones of any collective national identity and it is to them that I shall now turn.

As a result of the Elementary Education Act of 1870, literacy in England began to spread across the social scale. The legislation aimed to educate those recently enfranchised in the 1867 Reform Act and to meet the challenge of commercial competition from abroad. Between 1870 and 1880, when attendance was made compulsory to the age of thirteen, over three thousand schools were set up or taken over by school boards.

All over Europe nation states set about codifying a single printed vernacular and compiling a canon of literary texts which would frame a national literature: a shared language was seen as central to the creation of nationhood. In 1880, the academic discipline of English language and literature barely existed; yet by 1920 it was seen as an essential constituent of any national system of education. Although a professor of English language was established at University College London as early as 1828, it was not until the close of the Victorian period that the ancient universities, bulwarks hitherto of the classical tradition of Greek and Latin, began to respond. In 1890, English was separated from other languages in the new Cambridge tripos and four years later Oxford established an English School. In 1907, the English Association was founded to propound the new discipline, which was billed as 'our finest vehicle for a genuine humanistic education', and by the close of the 1930s it had achieved its objective of a unified written and spoken English being at the heart of the national curriculum. In this manner, the study of English language and literature slowly began to replace that of Greek and Latin; by the close of the twentieth century, knowledge of neither of the latter was required to secure entrance to the ancient universities.

But such a replacement of the classics presupposed

a canon of literary works in the vernacular that stood comparison with the literature of antiquity. This process of creating a national literature had already begun with Francis Turner Palgrave's (1824–97) *Golden Treasury of the Best Songs and Lyrical Poems in the English Language*, which appeared in successive editions from 1861. Palgrave's aim was to teach 'those indifferent to the Poets to love them, and those who love them to love them more'. Arranged chronologically and divided into four books, it reflected 'the natural growth and evolution of our Poetry'. Then, in 1900, came *The Oxford Book of English Verse*, which was to run through twenty editions by 1939 and still remains a touchstone for vernacular poetry today. Supported by the first serious multi-volume history of the nation's literature, *The Cambridge History of English Literature* (1885–1900), these anthologies established a poetic canon which conjured up a heroic national past and a civilisation whose heartland was the countryside.

This new academic discipline opened up the literary past, making available to a large audience Anglo-Saxon and medieval texts, such as *Beowulf* and *Sir Gawain and the Green Knight*, which had hitherto been the province of limited editions published by learned societies. A crucial role in this was played by the Early English Text Society, founded in 1864 by Frederick Furnivall (1825–1910), who had a lifelong passion for editing historic and literary texts that could shed light on the nation's cultural and social past. He also established the Chaucer Society (1868), the Ballad Society (1868) and the Wyclif Society (1882). In all this, the emergence of the English language was presented in parallel to the evolution of the nation's political and legal system, confirming the country's triumphal progress.

In the process Irish, Scots and Welsh literature were valued not in their own right but as somehow contributing to the rise and triumph of English. Although a chair of Celtic literature was established at Oxford in 1877, it was less evidence of recognition than of assimilation – completing a process that had begun as early as the reign of Edward I. English had been made the governing language of Wales in 1536, of Ireland in 1537 and of Scotland in 1616. In his book *Culture and Anarchy* (1869), Matthew Arnold had advocated the swallowing up of what he regarded as 'provincial nationalisms' by assigning them subsidiary roles as contributors to English literary culture over the centuries.

The creation of a national canon also called for the standardisation of language and its pronunciation. The landmark project here was the *New English Dictionary*, which began under the aegis of the Philological Society in 1857 but in 1879 passed to Oxford University Press and was henceforth known as the *Oxford English Dictionary*. Frederick Furnivall was again one of the driving forces behind what was clearly a nationalist agenda, for he and his fellow editors 'set ourselves to form a National Portrait Gallery, not only of the worthies, but of all the members, of the race of English words which is to form the dominant speech of the world'. The aim was to produce a single national language.

Sir James Murray (1837–1915) – a Whig, a Scot and a dissenter – became the dictionary's editor. In the preface to the first volume, which appeared in 1888, he expressed the hope that 'by the completeness of its vocabulary, and by the application of the historical method to the life and use of words, it might be worthy of the English language and of English scholarship'. In the eleventh edition of the *Encyclopaedia Britannica*, he presented his view that

> this evolution [of the language] appears so gradual in English that although we can nowhere draw distinct lines separating its successive stages we recognise these stages as merely temporary phases of an individual whole, and speak of the English language, as used alike by Cynewulf, by Chaucer, by Shakespeare, and by Tennyson.

Entries on individual words drew heavily on their use and appearance in works which had been accorded a place in the literary canon, thereby giving the language a somewhat illusory cohesiveness. That canon excluded the work of living writers; as the literary scholar Sir Sidney Lee (1859–1926) put it: 'Current writing which awaits the final verdict does not claim the attention of the lecture room.'

At the same time we witness the standardisation of pronunciation. The correct form of spoken English could only be identified by consigning diversity and regional dialects to the past. Henry Cecil Wyld (1870–1945), Merton Professor of English Language at Oxford, identified it as the English that was spoken in the country's great institutions: the Court, the Church, the Law, Oxford and Cambridge and the public schools.

All of this brought into fashion a distinctly masculine style in writing. The Oxford historian E. A. Freeman (1823–92) believed that the true roots of an English literary style were to be found in Anglo-Saxon. Its distinguishing marks he categorised as 'honesty . . . manliness and simplicity'. Freeman fervently believed that other languages were 'unmanly' and that words derived from both Latin and French were effeminate and should be purged.

The nation's dramatic heritage, above all the plays of Shakespeare, was also accorded institutional status. Shakespeare was regarded as the linchpin of England's language and literature, a man whose works enshrined universal truths and epitomised the virtues of compromise, humanity, nobility and national unity. What was to become the Royal Shakespeare Company opened in Stratford-upon-Avon in 1879, and it was also during the 1870s that plans to establish a National Theatre were first articulated – although this would only come to fruition after the Second World War. The apotheosis of Shakespeare as a central figure in the national mythology had been pioneered in the eighteenth century by the actor David Garrick (1717–79), so the playwright entered the Victorian age already as a national cultural treasure; being a Warwickshire man from a market town, he also fitted neatly into the new ruralist definition of England. The poet John Masefield (1878–1967) wrote in 1911 that Shakespeare was 'the greatest thing ever made by the English mind'.

Shakespeare's poetry had been included in Palgrave's *Golden Treasury* and *The Oxford Book of English Verse*. Now the so-called Georgian poets, a group that included Robert Bridges (1844–1930) and Walter de la Mare (1873–1956), celebrated the English rural idyll. Romantic, at times sentimental, but always patriotic, their poetry eulogised the countryside and its traditions; it would have an extraordinary hold over the national imagination during the two world wars.

Two instances must suffice here to demonstrate the power of their poetry. In 1896, the classical scholar A. E. Housman (1859–1936) published a collection of sixty-three lyrics entitled *A Shropshire Lad*. In simple and direct language it dealt with love, war and death in the Welsh Marches and anticipated with incredible foresight the tragedy of the First World War:

On the idle hill of summer
  Sleepy with the flow of streams,
For I hear the steady drummer
  Drumming like a noise in dreams.

Far and near and low and louder
  On the roads of earth go by,
Dear to friends and food for powder,
  Soldiers marching all to die.

But the poet who came to symbolise a whole generation of golden youth doomed to die was Rupert Brooke (1887–1915). First published in 1921, his collected poems had sold 100,000 copies by 1932. His five war sonnets were written not long before his death in 1915 and they include these famous lines from 'The Soldier':

If I should die, think only this of me:
  That there's some corner of a foreign field
That is for ever England. There shall be
  In that rich earth a richer dust concealed;
A dust whom England bore, shaped, made
     aware,
  Gave, once, her flowers to love, her ways
     to roam,
A body of England's, breathing England's
     air,
  Washed by the rivers, blest by suns of home.

Doomed golden
youth: Rupert Brooke

That same year Brooke wrote of himself in the third person:

> He was immensely surprised to perceive that the actual earth of England held for him a quality which, if ever he'd been sentimental enough to use the word, he'd have called 'holiness' . . . He felt the triumphant helplessness of a lover.

It is hard not to be moved by such intensity of feeling vocalised in the face of the country's possible defeat. Yet we should also note here that the ruralist vision that we find in Brooke and the other war poets could be put to the service of national and imperial goals in times of war. The two traditions would intertwine again during the Second World War: the rural vision of England once again became the touchstone of patriotism.

If England's language and literature were investigated and categorised, so the nation's past was recast as a panorama of stirring events and heroic characters which could draw a nation together with a sense of shared pride. The country's history was presented as one long pageant of progress.

This optimistic outlook shouldn't surprise us. After all, Victorian England could take pride in its vast economic wealth, its social stability and democratic institutions, its progressive extensions of the franchise and its ever-expanding empire. Henry Thomas Buckle (1821–62), in his influential *History of Civilization in England* (1857–61), cast the English intellect 'from the sixteenth to the eighteenth century as shaped by the growth of scepticism, toleration and liberty'. England's superiority went back as far as the Norman Conquest when circumstances 'began to affect our national character, and had assisted in imparting to it that sturdy boldness . . . those habits of foresight, and of cautious reserve, to which the English mind owes its leading peculiarities'.

This Whig interpretation of history remained popular. As late as 1945 the historian Herbert Butterfield (1900–79) could write in the aftermath of victory over Nazi Germany:

> Let us praise as a living thing the continuity
> of our history . . . reconciling continuity with
> change, discovering mediations between past
> and present, and showing what can be achieved
> by man's reconciling mind . . . Perhaps we owe
> most in fact to the solid body of Englishmen,
> who throughout the centuries have resisted
> the wildest aberrations, determined never for
> the sake of speculative ends to lose the good
> they already possessed: anxious not to destroy
> those virtues in their national life which need
> long periods of time for their development; but
> waiting to steal for the whole nation what they
> could appropriate in the traditions of monarchy,
> aristocracy, bourgeoisie and church.

As Mr Podsnap explained to a foreign gentleman
in Charles Dickens's *Our Mutual Friend* (1864–5): 'We
English men are Very Proud of our Constitution, Sir.
It was Bestowed Upon Us by Providence. No other
Country is so Favoured as This Country.' The Anglo-
Saxons now replaced the ancient Britons as the source
of England's democracy: the fount of English liberties
was located in the free moot of the Anglo-Saxon
village. In his *View of the State of Europe During the
Middle Ages* (1818), Henry Hallam (1777–1859) had
praised the Saxon period's 'free soccage tenants or
English Yeomanry, whose independence has stamped
with peculiar features both our constitution and our

national character'. In effect, the nations of the Celtic fringe were dismissed from this story of democratic evolution.

The great historian Thomas Babington Macaulay (1800–59) wrote in his *History of England* (1849–55): 'Our liberty is neither Greek nor Roman; but essentially English. It has a character of its own . . .' For him, the nation's modern history began in 1688 with the Glorious Revolution, which exiled a Catholic autocratic king, James II, and brought in the Protestant William III and the subsequent Bill of Rights. This long triumphal period would later include the massive extension of the franchise in the Second Reform Act in 1867; the Parliament Act which truncated the power of the Lords in 1911; and further extensions of the franchise, first to all men and then to women, in 1918 and 1928.

In the late Victorian era, constitutional history was established as a new academic discipline under the aegis of its two greatest exponents, William Stubbs (1825–1901) and Frederic Maitland (1850–1906). The latter wrote: 'Constitutional history should, to my mind, be a history not of parties, but of institutions, not of struggles, but of results; the struggles are evanescent, the results are permanent.' Such a benign interpretation of the English past – unfolding over the centuries and bringing free citizens, free markets, free trade, free religion and free enterprise – appealed to virtually every shade of political opinion at the time. It was unashamedly Anglocentric but we must remember that historians of the period wrote primarily for an English readership. J. R. Green's (1837–83) *Short History of the English People* (1874), which sold 32,000 copies in the first year of publication and remained in print well into the following century, is a good case in point.

There were other monuments to this newly found Anglocentricity. One was the English obsession with portraits. The National Portrait Gallery, although established in the 1850s, finally opened its doors in the present building off Trafalgar Square in 1896. There was to be a subordinate gallery in Edinburgh but nothing impinged on the metropolitan gallery presenting the island's history in terms of its people, most of whom were English. The majority of those who made it into the *Dictionary of National Biography*, published in sixty-three volumes between 1885 and 1900, also came from the southern parts of the island. The criteria of selection were the same as for inclusion in the National Portrait Gallery: the focus was on politicians, establishment figures and some eminent 'foreigners' who, like Holbein, had either worked or lived in England. The representation of women was negligible; as Sir Sidney Lee, who had become the dictionary's editor in 1891, wrote: 'Women will not, I regret, have much claim on the attention of the biographer for a very long time to come.'

These elements of the Whig interpretation of history would come together in the work of one of England's greatest historians, George Macaulay Trevelyan (1876–1962). Publishing his *English Social*

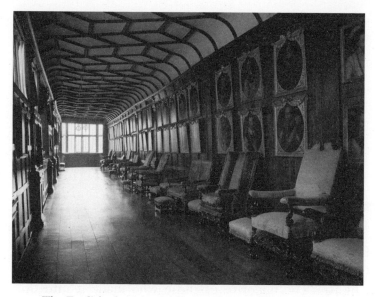

The English obsession with portraits: a gallery at Knole.

History (1944) as the Second World War drew to its
close, he believed passionately that the English countryside was the repository of England's identity, its liberty
and 'spiritual identity'. In the words of the historian Sir
David Cannadine:

> Trevelyan presented his readers with a
> beguiling picture of the past life of the nation,
> by turns inspiring and nostalgic. Written in
> the darkest years he had known, he poured out
> his patriotic feelings for what seemed to him
> the mortally endangered fabric of English life:
> landscape and locality, flora and fauna, places

and people. Out of his wartime sense of despair and foreboding, he created his final masterpiece of public enlightenment . . .

Language, literature and history were the foundation stones for a wide preoccupation with Englishness during the late Victorian and Edwardian period. The new interest in English history also led to a fascination with folklore. The Folklore Society was founded in 1878, but the most significant impact was made in the realm of music by Cecil Sharp (1859–1924). In 1899, Sharp had encountered a group of morris dancers and noted down the tunes they played. That awoke in him a passion for English folk song and music so consuming that within four years he had collected some 1,500 pieces. His influence was such that his work not only led to the revival of morris dancing – a tradition that had been dying out at the end of the nineteenth century – but to the education authorities laying down in 1914 that folk song be taught in the schools.

But Sharp's rediscovery of English folk music was only one aspect of the quest for the country's musical past. Sharp himself summed up the musical scene in 1907 in his *English Folk Song: Some Conclusions*:

Since the death of Purcell (1695) . . . the educated classes have patronised the music of the foreigner, to the exclusion of that of the

The English folk tradition revived.

Englishman. Foreign vocalists singing the foreign tongue, have for two centuries monopolised the operatic stage; while English concert platforms have, during the same period, been exclusively occupied by alien singers and instrumentalists singing and playing compositions of European writers.

The closing decades of the previous century had witnessed a musical renaissance. The landmark performance in this respect was Sir Hubert Parry's (1848–1918) *Blest Pair of Sirens*, a setting of Milton's poem 'At a Solemn Music' (found in Palgrave's *Golden Treasury*), composed to mark the Golden Jubilee of Queen Victoria in 1887. More important still, beginning with Sir Edward Elgar's (1857–1934) *Enigma Variations* (1899), a steady stream of composers drew on English poetry and literature for their inspiration, above all Ralph Vaughan Williams (1872–1958) and Benjamin Britten (1913–76). The age was also fascinated with the music of Tudor and Stuart England. In 1899, *The Fitzwilliam Virginal Book*, a treasure trove of Tudor music, was published; in 1913, E. H. Fellowes (1870–1951), a minor canon at Windsor, edited sixty-eight volumes of the work of the English madrigal school, which joined twenty volumes of the music of William Byrd.

The musical renaissance owed much to the foundation of a whole series of new institutions: the Royal College of Music (1882), the Royal Choral Society (1871), Henry Wood's Queen's Hall Orchestra (1896) – becoming the London Symphony Orchestra in 1904 – and, of course, the famous Henry Wood Promenade Concerts which began their annual life at the Albert Hall in 1895.

Yet over it all towers the figure of Sir Edward Elgar. For over two decades he was the major figure on the English musical landscape until, in the aftermath of the First World War, he fell from critical and popular favour. The composer of a wide range of works – from the oratorio *The Dream of Gerontius* (1900) to his Symphony No. 1 in A Flat (1908) – he also produced a steady stream of ceremonial and celebratory music

The epitome of the revived English musical tradition.

which has become part of English identity: above all the *Pomp and Circumstance Marches* and the *Coronation Ode* of 1902, the latter containing within it what is in effect England's alternative national anthem, 'Land of Hope and Glory'.

Tudor and early Stuart music, together with folk song, had a determining influence on Ralph Vaughan Williams, who unhesitatingly described himself as an English composer. His passionate concern with English national identity found expression in works such as his *Fantasia on a Theme by Thomas Tallis* (1910) and the song cycle based on the work of Housman, *On Wenlock Edge* (1909). In his capacity as musical director, he was also responsible for the incorporation of folk song into *The English Hymnal* (1906), which is still used in churches today. In his vocal works he used texts from the Bible, Shakespeare and William Blake. His oeuvre, like that of so many others from that period, fell from favour in the 1950s when there was a backlash against what was regarded as cultural insularity. Yet at that time Benjamin Britten would continue to make use of a network of essentially English icons – the country house, the village, the England of Elizabeth I and Shakespeare – in works such as *Peter Grimes* (1945), *Albert Herring* (1947), *Billy Budd* (1951), *Gloriana* (1953), *The Turn of the Screw* (1954), *Noye's Fludde* (1958) and *A Midsummer Night's Dream* (1960).

Finally, what is now the Royal Ballet began in 1931 as the Vic–Sadler's Wells Opera Ballet Company, whose style was set by Dame Ninette de Valois (1898–2001) and the choreographer Sir Frederick Ashton (1904–88). Its first major production was *Job* (1931) with music by Vaughan Williams and sets based on William Blake's illustrations. Diaghilev had rejected the proposal for such a ballet as 'too English', and other productions were equally English: Ashton's *The Lord of Burleigh* (1931) drew on Tennyson, de Valois's *The Rake's Progress* (1935) was inspired by Hogarth's pictures, Helpmann's *Comus* (1942) was based on Milton's masque and the patriotic plot of Ashton's *The Quest* (1943) drew on Book

One of Spenser's *The Faerie Queene.* After the war, when the company triumphantly moved to the Royal Opera House, that English bias began to fade – although Ashton's ballet *Enigma Variations* (1968), set to the music of Elgar, remains a testament to that tradition.

Another important development was the revival of English vernacular architecture, which began in the 1870s and drew on the buildings of Tudor England and those of the age of Queen Anne, which were bracketed together as 'Old English'. Recent scholarship attributes much of this impetus to George Devey (1820–86), who had studied the vernacular architecture of the Kentish Weald. In 1850, he designed a square of half-timbered and tile-hung buildings around the nucleus of a half-timbered house close to the church at Penshurst. These were to be architectural landmarks, from which descended the application of half-timbering to the between-the-wars suburban house. Devey became a prolific country-house architect, often remodelling old houses and estate buildings in this style.

His pioneering of the English vernacular was taken up by W. E. Nesfield (1835–88) and Richard Norman Shaw (1831–1912), who set up a joint practice in the 1860s and between them revolutionised English domestic architecture. They created the 'Old English' style with their use of stone, brick and half-timbering, massive chimneys, great halls, inglenook fireplaces and complex enveloping roofs. Earlier in the century 'Old English' had been a term used to describe both Tudor-Gothic and Elizabethan-style houses, but Nesfield's and Shaw's use of it epitomised a rejection of modern French and modern Gothic. In 1868, Shaw designed what was recognised as the milestone for the 'Old English' style, Leys Wood in Sussex. The architectural historian Mark Girouard explains why it caused such a furore at the time:

> It was designed as a cluster of different elements and roofs of different heights around a courtyard. Leaded lights and plate glass, large windows and small ones under the eaves, high rooms and low rooms were skilfully mixed up together. Under the blanket of 'Old English' it drew on a number of different periods and strata, with Gothic arches, Tudor windows, seventeenth-century chimney-stacks, half-timbering and tile-hanging artistically sprinkled with panels of sunflowers and other aesthetic trimmings. Inside, that picturesque feature of yeoman homesteads, the inglenook, had been brought up to date . . . the recipe was new and took the country, or at least the home counties, by storm. 'Old English' had been put on the map; and 'Old English' meant, not the imitation of a style, but the creation of an atmosphere.

A new ideal: the country cottage.

This eclectic view of Old England ennobled the black-and-white timber-frame house as much as it beatified the humble country cottage, seen to enshrine the domestic virtues of an earlier, more gentle, pre-industrial age. Helen Allingham's (1848–1926) romantic watercolours of cottages and their pretty gardens in her *Cottage Homes of England* (1909) waved a wand over what were often little more than picturesque hovels. For Vita Sackville-West, the creator of Sissinghurst, the cottage garden was 'probably the loveliest type of small garden this country has ever evolved'. The fruit of the owner's labours, it was comfortable, relaxed and profuse, using quintessentially

English plants such as pinks, lavender, sweet williams, hollyhocks, Canterbury bells, pansies, Michaelmas daisies, phlox and every kind of herb. As we have seen in the last chapter, these cottage gardens were an inspiration to William Robinson, Gertrude Jekyll and Sir Edwin Lutyens, who framed what is still recognised today as the English garden style. The romanticisation of the cottage with its garden, the village and the English countryside as a whole we owe to the late Victorian era.

All the developments described in this chapter have to be understood within the context of universal education. It was through education that this 'second invention of England' entered the bloodstream of the nation; it was to be through the school syllabuses and textbooks that the new configurations of English language, literature and history were disseminated.

History teaching played a crucial role. The policy laid down by the Board of Education in 1909 instructed teachers to pass over periods of bad government like the reigns of Edward II and Charles II and the interminable squabbles of eighteenth-century politicians, and concentrate instead on the growth of representative institutions and advances in education and human knowledge. Its purpose was to instil in pupils a sense of belonging to a nation with a historic destiny. There was also the aim to arouse a sense of national consciousness through the study of set texts, like Shakespeare's plays or Milton's *Comus*. The late Victorian era saw the creation of new state schools, new universities and new public schools, while Oxford and Cambridge assumed a national role framing what literature and history should be taught.

It was no longer exclusively members of the landed and clerical classes who benefited from education. The new middle classes internalised this new Englishness and in their turn carried its ideals and preconceptions into their careers in public service and the professions. This reframing of the educational system led to a cult of manliness, which produced what people still recognise as the English gentleman. Members of the professional and business classes emerged as a caste which shared the same speech patterns, mannerisms, gestures and mode of dress; they were taught to be competitive, even aggressive, men of action who abided by the rules of the game, who were courteous on winning and gracious to those who had lost. They were chivalrous and romantic and, of course, excelled at all forms of sport.

It was also during this period that cricket became recognised as 'the national game', emblematic of England and its pre-industrial rural past with its immemorial tableau of the village green, church, manor house and cricket pavilion and its cast of squire, parson, gentlemen players and villagers. Taken up by the newly formed public schools, an almost mystic potency was attributed to the game in terms of character-building and training for leadership. In

'Vitaï Lampada' (1897), Sir Henry Newbolt (1862–1938) created a poem about a schoolboy cricketer who grew up to fight in Africa:

> There's a breathless hush in the Close to-night –
> Ten to make and the match to win –
> A bumping pitch and a blinding light,
> An hour to play and the last man in.
> And it's not for the sake of a ribboned coat,
> Or the selfish hope of a season's fame,
> But his Captain's hand on his shoulder smote –
> 'Play up! play up! and play the game!'

We finally come to one of the most influential developments of the age: the rise of the preservation movement that set out to save England's historic buildings and landscape. Preserving the past for the enjoyment of everyone played a crucial role in the reconfiguration of the country's identity in the late Victorian and Edwardian age. The movement gathered momentum in the 1870s when the state legislated for the first time on the preservation of antiquities in situ, yet three attempts to pass a National Monuments Preservation Bill all failed. The Society for the Protection of Ancient Buildings was formed in 1877 under the auspices of William Morris (1834–96), and its influence finally ensured the passing of the Ancient Monuments Protection Act in 1882. Much of this was driven by an agenda to provide access for all to a shared landscape and

The national game.

led to the foundation, by Octavia Hill (1838–1912) and Canon Hardwicke Rawnsley (1851–1920), of the National Trust in 1895. This was the first of a series of pioneering initiatives which essayed landscape preservation in the interests of everyone; it has never really been about urban preservation but about making England's green and pleasant land available to all in the democratic age. The creation of the green belt in the 1920s and '30s and the post-war National Parks only extended that equation of England and the countryside.

In this amazing collusion of aestheticism, pastoralism and patriotism, a vision of England was constructed at the end of the nineteenth and the beginning of the twentieth centuries. It was formulated, however, at a time when so much of what it apotheosised came under attack or went into terminal decline. Yet the sweeping social and political changes of the twentieth century eroded but never quite replaced this vision.

These were astonishing decades during which English culture and history as never before were investigated, defined, edited and institutionalised. It was a project that was both rural and backward-looking, rooted firmly in an imagined collective past. But it was a grand vision that believed every man, woman or child should know the nation's history and sample at least some of its greatest cultural achievements as a shared inheritance. Responding to an unprecedented broadening of the education system, it redefined England for the new democratic age.

Epilogue

England Redefined?

The rural and the imperial vision revisited.

FIFTY-THREE YEARS AFTER ANNIGONI painted the portrait of the queen with which I opened this book, the American photographer Annie Leibovitz portrayed Elizabeth II before her state visit to Virginia in 2007. Once again she stands silhouetted against a winter landscape, this time the gardens of Buckingham Palace; the cosmic glow in the sky reminds me of the 'Ditchley Portrait' of her predecessor and namesake. The queen is now in her early eighties, her hair white. But hers is still a commanding presence which calls for no attributes of power to enhance her: no crown, no jewels, no symbol of an order of chivalry. Like the Annigoni painting, the Leibovitz portrait still encapsulates the two aspects of England which I have described in this book – the rural and the imperial. Yet the imperial dimension, so evident in 1954, is undoubtedly more muted in the latter.

During the fifty years of the queen's reign the country has changed dramatically – in some ways beyond recognition. What is England in the twenty-first century? Which of the elements of our national identity that I have described remain relevant and valid?

Long after I had left the grammar school, one of my history teachers sent an exercise book of mine to me which she had kept, filled with my childish maps and drawings, diagrams, notes and little essays. Looking at it now I am struck by the fact that we learned about Islam as well as the coming of Christianity. Then there are the Anglo-Saxons, the Danes, the Norman Conquest, the development of the castle and manor, and my drawings of successive styles of architecture – Norman, Early English, Decorated, Perpendicular. It closes with the quarrel over who was to invest the bishops, with drawings of a crozier, ring, mitre and cope. All of that I had been taught and had taken in by the age of twelve in 1947.

The teaching of English then was solidly founded on the study of a succession of Shakespeare plays, culminating in *A Midsummer Night's Dream* and *The Winter's Tale*. At that stage I didn't enjoy them that much but I was converted to the bard when I was taken to see John Gielgud as Polixenes. I recall learning the poetry of Browning, Tennyson, the Georgians and Milton – *Samson Agonistes* in particular. There were no books at home and I would enjoy reading in the fullest sense only later, but for Ordinary Level we read Thomas Hardy's *The Mayor of Casterbridge* and *The Trumpet Major*. As there was no teacher who knew anything about music, this thankless task was assigned to one of the science teachers and never rose above choral singing or listening to the gramophone. What we heard and sang was within the Cecil Sharp tradition: English folk songs along with items by Handel and Thomas Arne. About the visual arts we learned nothing, and the prevailing view was that English painting, apart from Hogarth, Turner and Constable, had depended for its existence on a stream of foreigners such as Holbein, Van Dyck and Kneller. Yet whatever the shortcomings of the teachers, I became acquainted with a rich national heritage from which I learned about England.

I now realise that such teaching of English culture and civilisation as part of everyone's education was a transient phase. Today the transmission of that precious shared experience seems no longer a priority as greater emphasis is given in the school curriculum to environmental problems, classes in citizenship and gender issues. The attempt to instil in pupils some outline of their national past has been abandoned in favour of courses that focus on specialised periods like the Tudors, the Russian Revolution, the two world wars and the Holocaust. Moving across the centuries from one period to another, children are left with no sense of chronology nor any coherent narrative to explain their own country and their place within the nation's history. It is not surprising that by 2007 seven out of ten schoolchildren had abandoned history by the age of fourteen. It seems that anyone who wishes to find out about English culture, history and civilisation must do so largely outside the education system.

I cannot help but feel deeply saddened by the direction in which all this has gone. I have spent most of my life studying England's past. My public career as director of both the National Portrait Gallery and the Victoria & Albert Museum placed me at the centre of the English cultural scene for over two decades. In addition, I produced a steady flow of books, articles, and radio and television programmes, virtually all of which have dealt with aspects of the nation's history and civilisation. I am not ashamed to say that I feel passionate about England.

But increasingly English people are cut off from their roots during a period when, in the face of Celtic independence, they need them more than ever. While successive governments have endorsed the expression of Welsh and Scottish regional identity, English identity in an age of devolution has been largely ignored. Today we live in a multi-ethnic and multicultural society and the variety of cultural traditions has vastly enhanced the way we live our lives. But I also believe that an understanding of the history and traditions of England enriches the lives of anyone living in this country, regardless of their culture, religion or ethnic origin.

It seems that today the country's history is transmitted through the media. Radio and television programmes on our national history as well as historical novels are enjoyed by huge audiences hungry to discover their own past. Yet in effectively replacing the curriculum by providing the cement of national identity through programmes on history, archaeology and architecture, television has created a new imaginary England – in a sense it is the modern equivalent of Geoffrey of

England as seen by the world.

Monmouth's *British History*. The nation's past is re-enacted through the dramatisation of Tudor history and the adaptation of the novels of Jane Austen, the Brontës, George Eliot, Charles Dickens and Anthony Trollope. Many of the great classics of our literature are now transmitted less by actual reading than by television; in turn these productions, sold around the world, influence how England is perceived by a global audience. They all present viewers with the mythological picture of a rural England of country houses, rectories, villages and churches. It is the world of Agatha Christie, *Midsomer Murders* and *Downton Abbey* – and it demonstrates the enduring power of the rural vision.

Yet this shouldn't surprise us, as the England defined in the late Victorian and Edwardian period has today behind it the full force of government legislation ensuring that the countryside and its historic-built environment are preserved. The last century witnessed an unprecedented effort by both government and independent bodies to protect, conserve and restore the country's natural and architectural heritage. The Council for the Protection of Rural England (founded in 1926) campaigns vigorously for the preservation of the countryside, and the National Trust now owns a huge section of our most cherished landscape and coastline, not to mention a galaxy of historic country houses and gardens. To these we can add the great National Parks, created by Act of Parliament in 1949, and the body responsible for hundreds of historic sites in its owner-ship that became English Heritage in 1983. All of this reflects an appreciation of the beauty and originality of English nature and architecture.

But we must remember that the pastoral vision of England which began to take shape in the 1880s was selective. For one, it didn't include London. This vast engulfing metropolis has always been a world apart, even in the Middle Ages, when Italian, German, French and Flemish merchants thronged the quaysides and had their own quarters in the city. London has always been cosmopolitan: it absorbed Protestant exiles from France and Flanders in the sixteenth and seventeenth centuries, Jews fleeing persecution in Russia in the nineteenth, those claiming British citizenship as members of our defunct empire in the twentieth and, most recently, those nationals from other European member states who have decided to live and work in Britain.

Moreover, as we have discovered, the rural vision of England is firmly rooted in the old Anglo-Saxon kingdoms of the South. The North, the country that stretches beyond York and up to the Scottish Border, has been fought over throughout history and tensions between the two parts of the kingdom remain; we only need to remember the confrontation between the miners' union and Margaret Thatcher in the 1980s. While cathedral cities like York, the Lake District and the cosy world of Beatrix Potter sit comfortably with the southern idyll, the North has retained its own identity which calls for tact and respect. We need to keep these important qualifications in mind when we embrace the rural vision as the key source of the nation's identity.

So which of the icons and traditions I have portrayed in this book still speak to us today? Which of them still endure, albeit transmuted? What can be passed on with a sense of collective pride and what has disappeared – sometimes, in my view, with great regret?

Of the two mythologies, pastoral and imperial, the twenty-first century is more in tune to the rural vision than to the idea of empire. Imperial glory has long gone; now England is just one of the many countries that make up the European Community. From time to time the imperial flame flickers, lit by wars in the Falklands, Iraq and Afghanistan, but our dogged belief in some 'special relationship' with the United States gives us delusions of importance which are quite unwarranted. I believe we have to face up to the truth that we are the inheritors of an idea of empire that no longer has any substance in reality.

Of the touchstones of national identity that originated in the Elizabethan period, the Church of England is still there – albeit seemingly forever in crisis and with a communicant membership of below a million. Today it seems that an understanding of even the barest outline of the Christian faith can no longer be taken for granted. The King James Bible and the Prayer Book have little relevance to most people below the age of fifty; in fact, art galleries and museums now find themselves having to explain the context of a picture that, for example, depicts the Crucifixion. I fear that future generations will be even less intellectually equipped to understand a good part of both European and English civilisation that is an expression of the Christian faith – a tissue of ideas and beliefs that has created our places of worship, graveyards and almshouses, and which pervades our poetry, prose, drama and music.

And yet in times of crisis – in the event of a national tragedy or when soldiers are brought home for burial from the field of battle – and on occasions of national thanksgiving and celebration, the Church of England and its clergy respond to a spiritual yearning to produce rituals and ceremonies which unite the English people. Indeed, the genius of the Church of England lies in its ability never to close its doors but to open them willingly to both the God-fearing and the godless. The Anglican Church remains a uniting force, and by its unquestioning inclusiveness still fulfils the role envisaged for it by its founder, Elizabeth I, in the sixteenth century.

Our Christian heritage also includes our great cathedrals, such as the glories of York, Durham and Canterbury, still visited by tens of thousands each year. More important still, there are our humble village churches, thousands of them dotted through the landscape, their towers and spires signalling from afar a settlement, each building speaking of centuries of human life and endeavour and each a manifestation of the continuity of English country life.

The monarchy too still occupies a crucial role in defining England. As I write, we approach the end of the reign of Elizabeth II, one likely to be even longer than that of Victoria and which has given the country an unparalleled sense of stability and continuity. The present queen has seen the empire become the Commonwealth and she remains queen of Australia, New Zealand and Canada – but the likelihood of that arrangement surviving in the next reign is uncertain. Equally, after devolution, the situation within the United Kingdom might call for adjustment. The position of the monarchy as a uniting force is as strong as ever, but decisions may have to be made as to its role in each of the countries that still form Britain.

The first Elizabethan era cast itself as a *renovatio*, a new beginning. This was England's spring: a time of excitement, energy and optimism. It could be argued that the greatest disaster that befell England's history – and affected its identity – was the accession of the Stuarts which led to the three kingdoms, a terrible civil war and after 1707, in the words of the historian Linda Colley, to the forging of a nation of Britons. The union weakened and distorted the second definition of England in the late nineteenth and early twentieth centuries; it bloated national identity with imperial mythology and injected it with an assumed superiority over Scotland and Wales.

The vision that emerged at that time has more than a touch of the autumnal about it. So much of this second definition was not only inward- but backward-looking: it lacked the balance between past, present and future that had informed the Elizabethan idea of England. The creation of a canon of national literature which excluded the present made it sterile; the Whig interpretation of English history, portraying the nation's past as an endless triumphal progression to the perfection of the present, became brittle once the nation and its empire began their long decline. In short, it was a definition which could only ever be sustainable as long as England was, as it were, on top of the world.

Such assumed superiority should no longer inform the sense of ourselves as a nation. Yet at the heart of the pastoral vision which emerged at that time lies much that is still part of the England of the imagination – *not* the England of reality, as this book has tried to elucidate. I have traced how England has always been defined by its countryside: the Industrial Revolution was effectively written out of the nation's identity. The Arcadian vision of an idealised rural life was incompatible with the reality of factories and furnaces, slums and human degradation.

Yet this shouldn't really surprise us. Identity always exists in the imagination and nations, in the scholar Benedict Anderson's famous phrase, are 'imagined communities'. But as far as imagined communities go, the rural vision of England strikes me as an attractive one. It is peaceful and tranquil; it speaks of a society that exists in harmony and where life follows the cycle of the seasons; and it respects and preserves the natural environment. It is, in Shakespeare's immortal words, 'This other Eden, demi-paradise'. It is a corrective to the speed and greed of urban life and an aspiration to those who are longing to escape the hustle and bustle of our big cities.

That rural idyll is still embraced by the millions who every year visit our National Parks, our country houses and their gardens, and those sections of our countryside that have become iconic, such as the Lake District and Constable's Suffolk; who take enjoyment from our great landscape art and the novels and poems that celebrate country life; and, last but not least, by all those who find pleasure in their allotments and gardens.

This is not a grand political vision – and it carries no nationalist fervour – but one could argue that it is quietly political: it speaks of humanity at peace, mutual respect and obligation, and life in harmony with the natural world. In its passion for the environment, it is a vision that is today more topical than ever. More important still, it is democratic and inclusive: I believe that it can be embraced and enjoyed by anyone living in this country.

The purpose of this book has been to remind readers of what generations of English people have taken for granted as the ingredients of their national identity. The decision about which of those icons and traditions to reclaim, reformulate and enhance is theirs.

Elizabethan gold medal with a laurel tree symbolizing the inviolate
island. The legend translates as 'Not even danger affects it'.

Select Bibliography

Anderson, Benedict, *Imagined Communities: Reflections on the Origin and Spread of Nationalism*, Verso, 1983

Barczewski, Stephanie L., *Myth and National Identity in Nineteenth-Century Britain: The Legends of King Arthur and Robin Hood*, Oxford University Press, 2000

Brown, Georgia, *Redefining Elizabethan Literature*, Cambridge University Press, 2004

Clanchy, Michael T., *England and its Rulers 1066–1272*, Blackwell, 1983

Clark, F. H., *The English Landscape Garden*, Pleiades Books, 1948

Clarke, Catherine A. M., *Literary Landscapes and the Idea of John of Gaunt's Speech*, D. S. Brewer, 2006

Colley, Linda, *Britons: Forging the Nation 1707–1837*, Yale University Press, 1992

Colls, Robert, and Dodd, Philip (eds), *Englishness: Politics and Culture 1880–1920*, Routledge, 1986

Daniels, Stephen, *Fields of Vision: Landscape Imagery and National Identity in England and the United States*, Princeton University Press, 1993

Davies, R. R., *The First English Empire: Power and Identity in the British Isles, 1093–1343*, Oxford University Press, 2000

Deuchar, Stephen, *Sporting Art in Eighteenth-Century England: A Social and Political History*, Yale University Press, 1988

Gervais, David, *Literary Englands: Versions of Englishness in Modern Writing*, Cambridge University Press, 1993

Grant, Alexander, and Stringer, Keith J. (eds), *Uniting the Kingdom? The Making of British History*, Routledge, 1995

Greenfield, Liah, *Nationalism: Five Roads to Modernity*, Harvard University Press, 1992

Hastings, Adrian, *The Construction of Nationhood: Ethnicity, Religion and Nationalism*, Cambridge University Press, 1997

Helgerson, Richard, *Forms of Nationhood: The Elizabethan Writing of England*, University of Chicago Press, 1992

John Piper, Tate Gallery exhibition catalogue, 1983

Knapp, Jeffery, *Shakespeare's Tribe: Church, Nation and Theater in Renaissance England*, University of Chicago Press, 2002

Kriz, Kay Dian, *The Idea of the English Landscape Painter*, Yale University Press, 1997

Kumar, Krishan, *The Making of English National Identity*, Cambridge University Press, 2003

Landscape in Britain c.1750–1850, Tate Gallery exhibition catalogue, 1973

Landscape in Britain 1850–1950, Tate Gallery exhibition catalogue, 1983

MacEachern, Claire, *The Poetics of English Nationhood 1590–1612*, Cambridge University Press, 1996

Maltby, Judith, *Prayer Book and People in Elizabethan and Early Stuart England*, Cambridge University Press, 1998

Matless, David, *Landscape and Englishness*, Reaktion Books, 1998

Morley, David, and Robins, Kevin (eds), *British Cultural Studies: Geography, Nationality, and Identity*, Oxford University Press, 2001

Murdoch, John, *The Discovery of the Lake District and its Uses*, Victoria & Albert Museum exhibition catalogue, 1984

Newman, Gerald, *The Rise of English Nationalism: A Cultural History 1740–1830*, Macmillan, 1997

Pevsner, Nikolaus, *The Englishness of English Art*, Penguin, 1964

Rosenthal, Michael, *Constable: The Painter and his Landscape*, Yale University Press, 1983

Samuel, Raphael (ed.), *Patriotism: The Making and Unmaking of British National Identity*, Routledge, 1989

Short, Brian, 'Images and Reality in the English Rural Community: An Introduction', in *idem* (ed.) *The English Rural Community: Image and Analysis*, Cambridge University Press, 1992

Tyacke, Sarah, and Huddy, John, *Christopher Saxton and Tudor Map-Making*, British Library, 1980

Vaughan, William, Barker, Elizabeth E., and Harrison, Colin, *Samuel Palmer 1805–1881: Vision and Landscape*, exhibition catalogue, Lund Humphries, 2006

Watson, Donald, *Shakespeare's Early History Plays*, Macmillan, 1990

Weiner, J. H., *English Culture and the Decline of the Industrial Spirit 1880–1980*, Cambridge University Press, 1981

List of Illustrations

Every effort has been made to trace and contact copyright holders. The publishers will be pleased to correct any mistakes or omissions in future editions.

Index